FAITH OF OUR FATHERS

FAITH OF OUR FATHERS

*African-American
Men Reflect on
Fatherhood*

EDITED BY
ANDRE
C. WILLIS

A DUTTON BOOK

DUTTON
Published by the Penguin Group
Penguin Books USA Inc., 375 Hudson Street, New York, New York 10014, U.S.A.
Penguin Books Ltd, 27 Wrights Lane, London W8 5TZ, England
Penguin Books Australia Ltd, Ringwood, Victoria, Australia
Penguin Books Canada Ltd, 10 Alcorn Avenue,
Toronto, Ontario, Canada M4V 3B2
Penguin Books (N.Z.) Ltd, 182–190 Wairau Road, Auckland 10, New Zealand

Penguin Books Ltd, Registered Offices: Harmondsworth, Middlesex, England

First published by Dutton, an imprint of Dutton Signet,
a division of Penguin Books USA Inc.
Distributed in Canada by McClelland & Stewart Inc.

First Printing, June, 1996
10 9 8 7 6 5 4 3 2 1

LIBRARY OF CONGRESS CATALOGING-IN-PUBLICATION DATA:
Faith of our fathers : African-American men reflect on fatherhood /
    edited by Andre C. Willis.
        p.   cm.
    ISBN 0-525-94158-4 (acid-free paper)
    1. Fatherhood—United States.   2. Afro-American fathers.
I. Willis, Andre C.
HQ756.F33   1996
306.874'2'08996073—dc20   95-48470
                                                                        CIP

Printed in the United States of America
Set in Palatino and Futura

To my father, Herbert,
and my sons, Clark and Coleman

ACKNOWLEDGMENTS

This project is all about family, friends, and community. It has been about reaching out, reaching in, reaching back, and reaching forward. It is, therefore, a project that seriously considers its sources—emotional sources, sources of memories, sources of sustenance, etc. With this in mind I would like to give many thanks.

My parents, Herbert and Helen Willis, should be acknowledged for their contribution to this volume ever getting off its feet. Without their care, the strength of my sister, Pamela Willis, and her daughters, Ashley and Alexandria, and the love of my cousins Kirby, Craig, and Brian Heyward, my aunt Jean Heyward, Uncle Oliver Luck, Uncle Randy, and Aunt Jena Luck, I could not imagine having the sense and stamina to see anything through.

In addition, the project would have never seen the light had it not been for the vision and good sense of Richard Newman of the W. E. B. Du Bois Institute at Harvard University. Randall Burkett, Peter Glenshaw, Carolyn MacLeod, Joanne Kendall, Sherry Lovelace, Jamal Gallow, and Diana Sterling were also helpful.

I owe a debt to the contributors, without whom none of this would have worked.

I would also like to thank the various students and faculty at Newton South High School, my students at Wesleyan University, Boston College, and Harvard University.

Jennifer Moore, my editor at Dutton, provided invaluable editing assistance and revolutionary patience. Susan Herner, my dedicated and talented agent, made the project worthwhile in more ways than one, and exhibited a profound link with and concern for the project that helped me to feel that it was a task worth the effort. For her dedication to the noble task of mothering, I also thank Karen Craddock.

Elleni and Corn showed me much love by loving each other and provided support in ways they will never know. I am in debt to them for sustaining me in times of great need. Sharon and Skip shine brightly as examples of happiness in the world and catalyze my own happiness through their smiles.

My friend from boyhood, Thomas W. Johnson, I deeply thank for doing whatever, whenever. Also, my inner-circle partners deserve a deep acknowledgment: Allen Payne for courage, creativity, and late-night dialogue; Craig R. Levine for critical discourse and friendship; Ronald E. Aubert for setting an example and providing assistance; Jalmus for thinking hard and swinging; Skayne for his discipline and commitment; Cook for his goodwill and intellectual audacity; William S. McFeely for his guidance and wisdom; Edward L. Jackson for nearby understanding and critical support.

Adam K. Mansbach provided invaluable assistance as

an editor on this text and as an interlocutor on various issues; to him I give a special thanks.

Yet, beyond the shadow of a doubt, I am most deeply indebted to Patricia Lorraine Rose for her unyielding support, incredible insights, inimitable courage, and incessant love as I have tried to accomplish not only the completion of this collection, but growth as a human. Consistently and daily, she has been an anchor in a sometimes stormy sea, a partner in an often turbulent world, a quiet voice in a soft moment, a smiling face and a strong companion in every possible context. Her ideas speak in me, her heart speaks to me, and all that comes through me is marked by her profound giving, love, and commitment. I thank her beyond thanks, and I graciously and gratefully watch our souls soar together.

CONTENTS

FOREWORD

by Alvin F. Poussaint, M.D.,
Clinical Professor of Psychiatry at
Harvard Medical School

This collection of essays by a distinguished panel of African-American men reflecting on fatherhood is as poignant as it is engaging. We read of the richness and diversity of experiences that black men share both as sons and fathers. These stories belie the stereotypes about black fathers. Here we have nurturing fathers, emotionally distant fathers, adoptive fathers, and, yes, absent fathers, too. These narratives also include reflections on the challenges of being a black father to biracial children. African-American fathers cannot be pigeonholed; their roles cannot be marginalized and restricted.

Nevertheless, the question of race is interlaced with the plots and subplots of these stories as they unfold within the context of the black American experience. It is clear that fatherhood for black men is an experience that both embodies and transcends the question of race. To love, nurture, discipline, and support one's child's growth requires a perspective that challenges the full scope of one's humanity. A black father can be good, bad, or anything in between. As these essays suggest, he can endure, rise above, or succumb to the malignant effects of racism. These authors experienced both joy and pain as they prepared their own children to face the perils (and the opportunities) that confront a black child in a white supremacist society.

The black men in this volume have achieved. There still, however, remain traces of the rage of a non-privileged class as they recite the impact of race on their own lives and families. No matter how high black men climb, they must still battle the traditional stereotypes and negative images of black masculinity, one of which is the demeaning public perception that they often fail in their fathering role.

Media images have dealt unfair and damaging blows to the black father's status. The portrayal of black males as irresponsible, out-of-wedlock and/or absent, hustling fathers who avoid gainful employment and sexually exploit women is widespread. Movies such as *The Color Purple* have embellished these stereotypes by depicting black fathers as one-dimensional macho clowns—brutal wife beaters who sexually abuse their children. Newspapers and magazines regularly reinforce objectionable father images with feature articles on the so-called "black underclass." African-Americans have felt shame, anger, despair, and guilt about these unflattering popular expositions.

The media picture, however, has not been entirely bleak. Bill Cosby, the star of the immensely popular television sitcom *The Cosby Show* and author of the national best-seller *Fatherhood*, has been dubbed "America's favorite father." Other current television programs present the black father as a solid family man. In the black community, many "big brother" mentoring programs organized by black fraternities and community groups to help black children stand in sharp contrast to the stereotype of the black male as a bebopping, street-wise, hyper-sexed individual who wants to make babies but wants no role in nurturing or supporting them. The Million Man March in Washington, D.C., brought together hundreds of thousands of black men who affirmed their responsibilities to their families and children. We have many reasons to feel proud about the overall performance of the black father while at the same time recognizing that there is reason for serious concern. As we try to grasp his current dilemmas, a brief look at the historical role of the black father is enlightening as well as reassuring.

It is well known, for instance, that the black father played a strong role in the West African societies from which most slaves were seized. African men were active in caring for children and protecting their families. These structures were profoundly disrupted by slave traders who split up families, bringing them to American shores to be brutalized like animals.

Black slaves struggled against great odds to maintain family structures. There were few single-parent, female-headed households during slave times. Often premarital intercourse and pregnancy, when it occurred, led to a settled, stable marriage. Men and women had a mutual interest in raising children and in sharing family responsibilities. Even though black men were often separated from their families by being assigned elsewhere or sold away, most maintained connections with their families. That the father was an important figure is indicated by the fact that children were frequently named (both first and last names) for their fathers rather than their mothers.

When slave fathers were physically separated from

their homes, there were other men who became "spiritual" fathers in the lives of the women and children left behind. Church deacons, male relatives, and friends stepped into the substitute father role and were given kinship designations such as "Pa," "Uncle," or "Grandpa." These strong kinship bonds were, at least in part, a continuation of African traditions.

The black father's strong involvement in his family continued after emancipation in 1863. Historians report that father-headed households were the norm in the 1880 census. Such households represented about 84 percent of black rural families and about 72 percent of black urban families. Significantly, historian Herbert Gutman states, "Fathers with unskilled occupations headed families just as regularly as fathers with either artisan skills or middle-class occupations."*

Gutman reported that in 1905 about 85 percent of New York City's black households were headed by men, despite brutal discrimination and emasculation through a variety of de jure and de facto racist actions. In 1925 in Harlem, five in six black children under age six lived in homes with both a father and a mother present. These facts indicate remarkable father commitment and stability when we consider that most black men were at the bottom of the economic scale in the most menial of jobs. Many scholars believe that Southern black migrants initially brought with them the strong kinship tradition of their Southern lifestyle, but that these traditions were slowly eroded under the often chaotic conditions in

* Gutman, Herbert. *The Black Family in Slavery and Freedom 1750–1925*. New York: Pantheon, 1975.

Northern urban ghettos (and, today, in Southern ones as well.)

By 1965, the Moynihan report ominously, yet also disparagingly, called attention to the problems of the black father. It reported that 25 percent of black families were single-parent, female-headed households. More alarmingly, by 1986—only twenty years later—the number of such households had increased two-fold! The awesome statistics tell their own story: more than 70 percent of black babies born in recent years have been born out of wedlock, and over 50 percent of black families are currently single-parent homes headed by women. What is happening to the black father?

Many civil rights leaders had hoped that with the demise in the 1960s of officially sanctioned forms of segregation and discrimination, black males would have greater access to the mainstream of American society and be in a better position economically, educationally, psychologically, and socially to sustain viable marriages and families. Instead, the overall situation has continued to deteriorate, particularly among the poor.

Most of this deterioration in the role of the black father is demographic and socioeconomic in origin and is not due to a so-called damaged psychological outlook on the part of black males, as some social scientists would have us believe. First of all, there is a shortage of black males to serve as fathers. There are about 85 black males for every 100 black females.* This discrepancy has many causes, including the fact that black men have a lower life

---

* Staples, Robert and Johnson, Leanor Boulin. *Black Families at the Crossroads.* Jossey-Bass: San Francisco, 1993.

expectancy than black women; many black males die at a young age from homicide, accidents, and suicide; many black men are in prison or are drug addicts; black men have a higher rate of severe mental disorder than black women; and an unknown number of black men are gay. It is estimated that there is only one available black male per five unmarried black females. If black males are an endangered species, then it follows that black fathers are endangered as well.

The ability and commitment of black men to serve in the fathering role has also been influenced by changing societal attitudes toward women, sex, and families. As segregation began to crumble in the late 1960s, women entered the work force en masse, displacing many black male workers. Simultaneously, the stagnant economy of the 1970s and the shift to new technology and service jobs left many black men without the education and skills to compete for any except the lowest-paying jobs. These problems are likely to continue because of high school drop-out rates today, which are 60 to 70 percent among black males in our largest cities. It is shocking that in 1960, 75 percent of all black males were employed, and in 1984, only 54 percent of black males were employed. Today, it is estimated that only 60 percent of black males are employed. This social tragedy accounts for a persistent black poverty rate of about 34 percent versus 12 percent among whites.

Though class differences by occupation do not necessarily predict a father's absence, the father with no occupation is another matter. The ability of a man with a subsistence job to contribute to the support of his family is very different from the situation of the jobless male who may not only feel economically inadequate to the task of maintaining a family but also may feel psychologically inadequate. Unemployed black men with low self-esteem are easily seduced into believing that manhood is gained by "making" babies rather than by raising them. Coupled with freer sexual lifestyles among the young, these circumstances are more likely to lead to out-of-wedlock births and fatherless homes. Male "chivalry," which often led to so-called shotgun weddings, has markedly diminished among our "liberated" youth, particularly if they are jobless.

Today, unemployment and underemployment among black males are the key factors contributing to the difficulty, if not the virtual impossibility, of maintaining the black male fathering role in the family structure. Financial instability also contributes significantly to a black divorce rate that is twice the white rate. And black women who divorce are considerably less likely to remarry than white divorcees, because of the shortage of black males.

Some sociologists speculate that the predicament of female-headed households feeds on itself as boys (and girls) raised in such families experience no models for marriage and fatherhood. "The failure of young black men and women to behave responsibly in the area of reproduction and child rearing represents a menace to the stability of black America unlike anything we have yet experienced," Playthell Benjamin warns in this volume.

Finally, a diminished interest in the parenting role among some black men may be due to society's general negligence in stressing the importance of the fathering role. Young men often do not know or understand just what a father's responsibilities are. Many, unfortunately, do not understand that fathers are relevant to a child's healthy growth and development, or that unemployed, separated, and out-of-wedlock fathers can also interact with their children and contribute significantly to their well-being. As Cornel West states in this volume, "The most important things for black fathers to try to do is to give of themselves, to try to exemplify in their own behavior what they want to see in their sons and daughters and, most important, to spend time with and give attention to their children. This is a big challenge, yet it is critical as we move into the twenty-first century."

Solutions to the black father's dilemma are difficult and complex, but the essays in this volume should contribute to the reestablishment of the black father's critical role in the black family and community, and, I hope, will engender more creative ways of supporting the black male in these roles. In the meantime, black men should strive whenever possible to serve as spiritual and psychological fathers to all black children who want and need them. "All parenting requires a certain degree of heroism. I struggle, and ask you to struggle, to be the superheroes we need to be" are the final wise words of contributor Thaddeus Goodavage, in this brilliant collection of essays, *Faith of Our Fathers*.

FAITH OF OUR FATHERS

INTRODUCTION

At least once a semester since they were infants, I have—sometimes when they really did not express an interest in going—taken my children to whatever course I was teaching. Fortunately, I have usually had solid child care available, so I rarely *had* to bring my kids with me. I just wanted them to have a broad range of early experiences, and I wanted to see how they would respond to seeing me in a primary role other than that of father. I would loosely bundle my firstborn up in blankets, place him in his car seat/infant carrier, and situate his sleepy six-week-old brain next to whatever lectern or table I was using. He would, like most of the students I was addressing, fall fast asleep.

As they got older and I got divorced, I would still bring both of my children to my classes. They would run around, engage students, practice their public-performance talents, provide comic relief, and, understandably, be distractions. Nevertheless, I am still committed to doing this at least once a semester because my students have made it clear that on the days I bring my kids they are able to see not only a different dimension of my personality, but also the different ways people interact with their children.

One of the most important, difficult, and heroic tasks in our society is to parent. Yet there is no space in our society in which to *critically* discuss what parenting is about. Bringing my children into the classroom catalyzes a type of critical discourse about parenting that is, quite simply, not happening in many other spaces. The dialogue that we have is frequently quite illuminating, and it highlights the need for deeper reflection and discussion about parenting, childhood, maleness, fatherhood, and how race affects one's understanding of these various issues.

After my most recent episode with my kids in the classroom, a young white woman student approached me to say that she had never seen an African-American man caring for young children. She therefore did not have any means to assess what she had seen in the class session with my children around—it was an entirely new experience for her. When I asked her how she imagined her African-American friends' relationships to their fathers, she claimed that she had never pictured them spending time alone as infants with their fathers, just with their mothers.

This, it seems to me, is an extreme case. Unquestionably, this well-intended and kind-hearted student was incredibly ignorant about the subject of black fathering. Yet this student, and the various other well-informed students who seem to ask somewhat ridiculous questions about black parenting, suggest there must be a deep deficiency in the representation of black fatherhood and a profound confusion about black masculinity. Moreover, the classroom dialogue underscores the fact that African-American men and women have important questions about black masculinity and fatherhood that are not being critically addressed and answered.

Black masculinity is too frequently represented, and thereby understood, as simply posturing as a gangster. This moment, deeply linked to the gangsterization of American society—that is, the commitment to amass power and control in whatever realm by any means one deems appropriate—is a sign of a wider cultural trend. Patriarchial, white supremacist America leaves individuals, particularly those in worse historical shape, less and less of an opportunity to express the fullness of their humanity. Black masculinity is understood in a narrow fashion (given the preponderance of negative images of black men), and black fatherhood is regarded as a surprising anomaly.

I bring my children to class as another way to engage about parenting and love, yet much more than this is required if we want to transform the prevailing conceptions of black masculinity and fatherhood.

My father taught me all about cars, lawn mowers, carpentry, baseball, etc. He handed down the wonderful conventionally male things that a father is supposed to give to his children. Even after all of his teaching, though, when I faced my newborn son I was radically unprepared. I did not know how to father. Or did I?

Being a father is at once intuitive, learned, and embedded in culture, history, class, and location. It is something one has to learn, yet it cannot be taught. This particular type of love from the particular location of father must come through you. It means setting examples, breaking stereotypes, loving hard, loving gently, sharing, being emotionally honest, considering, crying, fighting, kissing, holding, carrying, hugging, supporting, disciplining, pushing, probing, and wondering with a younger dependent soul striving for autonomy, self-esteem, and self-love. It is providing feelings of connection that sustain, yet feelings of support that are liberating. Being a father is a difficult and important task.

Looking back on my father now that I am a father has given me a much more informed perspective on our relationship. Dad struggled hard building himself, building a family, building a legacy. He built a lot and taught a lot, and I'm sure—even though he did not show me— he laughed a lot and cried a lot too. I always sensed his courage and never felt his fears. Now I understand him clearly as a man with certain flaws and many strengths, but when I was younger he was a towering figure. My dad never gave me explicit instructions on how to be a father, but he gave important examples that allow me to raise certain questions that impact me as a man today.

When one has a child, fatherhood both quickly slams and gently creeps into one's identity, and how we have seen fathers engage, how we have felt fathered, how we have heard fathers talk, how we have imagined fathers, all inform how we father. Most important, it seems to me now, is how the *faith of our fathers*—faith in us, faith in themselves, and faith in the world—has inspired how we want to live and want to love.

A major theme that runs throughout the grand history of Western literature is the investigation of the relationship between fathers and their sons. For example: the story of Abraham and Isaac in the Hebrew Bible; the quest of Telemachus for his father, Odysseus, in Homer's *Odyssey*; the protagonist Bazarov's nihilistic confrontation with his parents in Turgenev's epic novel *Fathers and Sons*; the tense father/son-centered plot in Shakespeare's *Hamlet*; the embittered relationship between Stephen and Simon in James Joyce's *Portrait of the Artist as a Young Man*; all the way up to the struggle between John and his father, Gabriel, in James Baldwin's powerful *Go Tell It on the Mountain*, all have provided us with complex questions and profound insights into this special bond. Even in music, art, and religion, the father-son relationship is a frequent theme. More recently, of course, many family discussions, community, club, and church dialogues, television shows and therapy sessions have been obsessed with the importance of father and son.

Yet, on the other hand, one could explain some of the attention given to the father-son relationship by understanding these variations inside the system that supports them —patriarchy. An implicit presupposition of patriarchy is that the father-son bond is critical to the maintenance and perpetuation of male dominance, and generations of men have depended on the sacred pact between father and son to sustain the great fallacy of male supremacy. Most of the discourse concerning the father-son link, however, even when it has demonstrated that patriarchal structures ultimately hurt everybody, has not examined the deeper implications of patriarchy. What is clear is that patriarchal conceptions of fatherhood require a type of emotional distance. A child wants comfort, tenderness, and closeness, but a patriarchal father is distant, hard, and unfeeling. This traditional role not only promotes an emotional disconnectedness between father and son, but also it emphasizes a false sense of gender differences that are constraining, in profoundly different ways, for men and women. But the system of patriarchy churns on.

In order to challenge patriarchy, however, we need not only to discuss ways in which it has been and continues to be problematic, but also examine how we can imagine changing our behavior in order that this system of gender dominance will not propagate itself further. This revolutionary shift stems from a combination of introspection, reflection on social forces, and a courageousness to engage the world in new ways.

The following collection of essays approach the father-son relationship from various angles. What connects them is the depth of their meditations, the integrity of their reflections, and the unwavering commitment to the hope that somehow the general quality of relationships between fathers and sons, and ultimately humans in general, can be improved. In this way the authors of these pieces are not merely contributors to a text, but to a vision.

None of the contributors have a particular commitment to studying parenthood or families. Yet they have all been fathered, in very different ways, some more "successfully" than others, according to their essays—and they each provide a passionate articulation of their experiences, an insightful comprehension of their interactions, and an inspirational account of their visions. None of them make explicit claims against patriarchy or white supremacy, yet their essays inspire the conscious reader to read between the lines to come to their own conclusions.

This collection was originally inspired by the assault on the humanity of black people. More specifically, it grew directly out of the misrepresentation of African-American men. In an image-obsessed society, with the disproportionate representation of black men as the stereotypical criminal and oversexed beast, the usefulness of this type of collection was clear. To the question of how can we counter problematic, stereotypical images of black men, this text responds with more substantive and real ones.

Yet this collection attempts to do something a bit deeper than counter images. These highly talented contributors were given an assignment that took them beyond the usual superficial rhetoric about being positive. They were asked to conduct sensitive yet critical investigations of parts of themselves and their families that are often hard to reveal. They were asked to dig in the graveyards of memory, look in hard places, and walk in emotional minefields. They were asked to shed an honest light on how African-American men must do their work as fathers, and they were asked to talk about being fathered. The most important statement they made after doing the digging, looking, and walking that raised many wonderful, difficult, and important issues and questions, was to still counter the pervasive stereotypes of black men. It's clear after reading these essays that without even trying to provide "positive" images and stories, this collection elevates black men. It lifts them up by clarifying their struggles, articulating their fears, and highlighting the complexity of their positions and visions.

Patriarchy and white supremacy are deeply, radically, and powerfully challenged by the following meditations on fatherhood. These African-American men, mostly academics, all writers, from various classes and hues, and different political vantage points, have laid a claim for black humanity that should softly reverberate for some time. I hope you enjoy it.

John Edgar Wideman

My Father's Son

John Edgar Wideman is a professor of English at the University of Massachusetts at Amherst. Among his books are the classic Brothers and Keepers, Philadelphia Fire, *and most recently,* Fatheralong. *He is currently at work on a new novel.*

There are at least two stories here. One about forgiving. One about forgetting. Very different stories seeming to need to be told at once. Time is what links them and distinguishes them and blurs the space of one into the other. Time and my father.

For fifty-one years I was my father's eldest son and then one day, in a moment, I wasn't. The news my father has another son older than I am, living somewhere on the same planet, a son I'd never heard of till the news was delivered by a total stranger over the phone, a woman who'd been the son's wife and had borne his children, this news shocked me, naturally, but also left me feeling, So what. I was, after all, a grown man, still my father's son, and I'd learned from him not to be surprised by anything. Anything could happen and surprising things often did and usually it was bad stuff and could shock the shit out of you, but you couldn't afford to act surprised, it was always too late for that and besides nobody's business if you were surprised so you didn't waste time with being surprised, certainly didn't show it, you just did what you had to do to get on with the business of what to do next.

So what, I was thinking even while she spoke. Why are you telling me this, lady?

I'd checked into a motel in Rochester, New York, a couple hours before my hosts from the Arts Council were scheduled to pick me up and take me to dinner. I owed them a performance after the meal and was looking forward to a little down time, relaxing before deciding what I might read to them later. It had been a busy fall. Two months on the road flogging a new book of stories, and when I'd pulled into the motel parking lot that afternoon, I'd realized how exhausted I was. Not by the drive from my home in Massachusetts as much as by the prospect of yet another night in yet another room with a number in yet another city where if I fell down and died in the street, I'd be yet another stranger for some stranger to have to step over or step around.

Two messages were waiting. The expected one from my hosts, welcoming me, confirming the pick-up time, leaving a phone number in case of emergency. The other message from a Janice Wideman—name, number, please call. I didn't know a Janice Wideman. My brother Dave had been married once to a Janet, but they'd been divorced for years and I hadn't heard from Janet for even longer than that. For some reason I was more than slightly curious about the message. Since I seldom managed to decide what I was going to read until I saw the whites of my audience's eyes, the shuffling among choices, each choice more painfully flawed and inappropriate the closer I pushed it to the brink, could wait till after I dialed Janice Wideman.

Thank you so much for calling, she said. A pleasant, clear, slightly anxious voice. I hoped you'd call, she said.

You don't know me but we know all about you. I got so excited when I read in the paper last week you were coming to Rochester. We plan to attend the reading tonight, but I really was hoping for a chance to speak with you beforehand. I called earlier and they said you weren't expected till after four. Left a message just in case. You see, even though you don't know us, we're family. I especially want the kids to see you, I showed them one of your books. We're all quite proud of you.

I'd like to believe someone in the audience remembers what I read that night in Rochester. I don't have a clue. After locating the family grouping which, based on her description, must be them—not difficult since they'd lined themselves up front row center—all I wanted was for the reading to be over. She'd told me enough over the phone to separate our rendezvous after the reading from all the other spontaneous encounters with Widemans I'd never met before, the ones clearly related and the ones not, the maybes, all the black people who'd turn up at book readings or signings across the country bearing the somewhat unusual, spelled as we spell it, Wideman name. Unusual unless you happened upon a source like the Greenwood, South Carolina, phone book, where we overflow two whole columns.

She'd said the man she'd married was my father's son. Their daughter accompanied her that evening in Rochester, along with two boys and a girl who were her daughter's kids. Grandmom, mom, the boys were brown, my color more or less, the little girl blue-eyed, a platinum blonde, skin pale as a Dürer angel.

Who were they to me. And who the hell was I, a couple of the questions knocking around in my head as I tried

not to stare when finally they took their turn at the podium, smiling, shaking hands with the visiting writer. If
I had it to do all over again today, I wish we'd be hugging
and kissing but nothing near that happened then.

A man somewhere, my age plus some months, my
father's son, and I'd never even dreamed he existed, but
here was his wife and two more generations to prove he
did.

Not much more said that night about who was related
to whom and how and why. Not in front of the kids, not
with strangers wishing me well and presenting books to
be autographed, my hosts hovering, anxious for the little
knot of folks to dissolve so they could hustle me to a
reception at the home of somebody on the Arts Council
board.

The woman I'd met over the phone was shy. Clearly
happy to see me in person and introduce her family, her
smile warm, eyes bright, manner unaffected and attractive, but none of it easy for her either. Was she measuring
my face for traces of his? Did the kids see him in this new
person they were greeting? She understood the potential
awkwardness for me. How I might have chosen, if I'd
been given the choice, to have none of this occur . . .

She said she'd write. Plenty of questions I couldn't ask
on that occasion crowded my eyes, I'm sure. For about
three minutes we stood alone enough to be specific, particular, exchange some information. Names. Dates. Places.
Yes, his daughter and grandkids and there were other children too. Doing well. Doing fine. I confirmed a few details
of my story. No doubt in her mind about the connection,
especially now, meeting me face to face, everything she'd
heard and read and pieced together fit perfectly, still, she

needed to hear me say some things, acknowledge facts she'd discovered on her own. A matter of me admitting them, perhaps. Saying words my father never had.

My father's first son lives in Michigan. My father hadn't married the mother of his first son, yet she had given the son my father's name, first, middle, and last. That's how this woman beside the podium was Janice Wideman. She'd been the one to raise the kids after her marriage to my father's son broke up. One daughter a sophomore in college. A son, I think she said, lives in the same town as his father.

She promised to write and tell me more. And did. Handwriting eerily similar to my mother's. On the dainty kind of note paper with matching envelopes my mother likes. Though the notion didn't make any sense, I couldn't help reading the letter as if my mother had written it, just as I couldn't stop finding my sister's features in the face of this woman who'd married my unknown half brother. I'd definitely been on the road too long. Experiencing the slippage, the loss of bearings that gradually strands you outside yourself. Too many scene shifts, changing faces, too much rushing around, too many performances, it all becomes an aimless, nonstop running in place. Nothing feels real. Who you are as arbitrary as where you are. The brick walls of a low-slung, tacky motel in Rochester, New York, where you're arriving to spend the night, interchangeable with a gleaming tower in L.A. where the publisher books you, both interchangeable with the one before, the one after, the next and next.

You know, you really had me going for a while there. Listening to you on the phone I didn't say it out loud but I was steady thinking. Whoa. Wait a minute. Who is this person claiming to be Edgar Wideman's wife? What is all this mess about? My mother's the one married to Edgar Wideman.

No way of telling that anybody's told you so I just jumped right in . . .

I have yet to respond to Janice Wideman's letter. For a good while afterward spoke only to my wife about what I had learned in Rochester. The *so what* part of my response in charge. Except I mentioned the surprise, the coincidence, how bizarre it all had been, to one of my hosts over breakfast the morning after the reading. A guy I'd liked instantly, who was easy to talk to. Who listened to the barest factual outline of what had transpired— phone message—revelation—meeting—without probing for more. He shook his head and said, Wow. Let me fold the rawness, the weirdness of it quickly into our casual conversation over coffee and Spanish omelettes, *specialty of the house*, in a little diner at the edge of downtown just before the interstate, where he'd led me to get a jump on rush-hour traffic when I headed back to Amherst that following morning.

He handed me my honorarium and said, Thanks for coming. The reading was great. Don't know how you managed to be so cool with the other business on your mind. Then said he was sorry and hoped I was okay. Must have been tough, he said. Not tough, I wanted to say. And of course not your fault. But I let it go. I'd said enough, probably more than I needed to say. I couldn't expect him to understand why sorry had nothing to do with anything. I had bounced what I needed to bounce off him. Told him just enough to put him in my shoes maybe a minute, maybe. I had no intention of going fur-

ther or of leaving him stranded in the middle of something, but that's exactly where I was—drifting in the middle of something, not able to say any more about it, and
guessed he might be the kind of person who wouldn't
need more talk from me to figure all that out.

My father's son. I'm talking about myself now. How my
father's in me. Not exactly leaving things unsaid, unex-
plained, but leaving things to explain themselves. As if
they can and should. As if it's enough. And if not, tough
shit. People will think what they want to think no matter
what you try to tell them. People listen only up to a point.
So what's the big deal. *So what.* After a point, there are
no explanations, only what happened, the silence following what happens and who could explain that. Who'd be
silly enough to try. Silence of years and distance. Who
could talk up reasons for that, to forgive or forget or make
sense of that. Silence.

Her letter's on my desk. Near the bottom of the pile of
correspondence I never get to the bottom of. Maybe
someday I'll write back. Or more likely, phone her. I'll
tell her some of what's happened since. How I spoke to
my father, then my mother about the man Janice Wideman married. One thing I know I'll ask her is the address
and phone number of her former husband, my brother,
half brother, whatever he is to me. I'll ask because I'll be
ready to contact him and I'm not ready yet and that
would also be my excuse for not writing sooner. I must
be ready. Now that I know *about* him, learning more before we meet feels unnecessary. I'm curious. But so what.
Curiosity's besides the point. Seems self-indulgent, almost unwholesome. A kind of prurient, one-way looking
without being seen. He's out there alive and breathing,

as far as I know, out there where he's been my entire life and some months more. Because I know he's out there, here, as real as I am, I can't play games. We're connected. Accumulating more facts about him changes nothing. Makes the connection neither more nor less certain.

The only answer to her letter is yes or no. You could say I've been holding my breath since her phone call in Rochester that fall afternoon three years ago. I know about him now. In the call, our meeting, her letter, she's told me more than enough. I've been holding my breath— no time, half a breath is all that's expired since her appearance that was both a statement and a question. My turn now to respond. Or rather say yes, if and when I'm ready to say yes, because I've been answering all along, haven't I, with silence, with no.

We are in South Carolina, my father and myself, in a rental car on a rural highway on our way to see Balus Glover, a black man nearly a hundred years old who everybody around here says is a living history book, the last of the old, old folks who might remember seeing my grandfather Harry or his father, the Reverend Tatum W. Wideman, driving his one-horse buggy, Mrs. Wideman perched beside him on the seat wearing one of the bonnets she never appeared in public without. It's a roots trip for my father and me, exploring this part of the country, the Piedmont region of the state where my grandfather was born and raised, where Widemans abound in the telephone book and church graveyards. We're just outside Promiseland, a community settled by former slaves around 1876. This is the second day of a week's visit down here, me fifty-one and my father twenty-one years older, our first trip together, just the two of us, as far as I recall, ever.

Hey, Dad. Need to ask you about something. A strange thing happened to me two years ago in Rochester, New York, of all places. A city I'd never been to before in my life. You ever been to Rochester. Huh-uh. Well, anyway, I met a woman there named Janice Wideman. She claimed to be Edgar Wideman's wife. I was pretty damned confused. Didn't know what the hell she was talking about. Then she explained her husband, the Edgar Wideman she married, was your son. First time I'd ever heard you had a son older than I am. But that's what she said. Boom. Out of the blue. I'm in a motel room in Rochester, New York, and suddenly some woman announces I have an older brother. Kind of a surprise, you might say.

Guess it was. Janice Wideman, you say. Huh-uh. Never heard of a Janice Wideman.

But the man she was married to. Him. Where she got our name. You know about him, don't you.

Suppose I would, wouldn't I. Mister. If it's who I think it might be, maybe I do. Know who he could be, anyway, but I've never laid eyes on him, myself.

There was a woman. She was around when your mother and I started getting serious. A girlfriend I'd been seeing. She left Pittsburgh before your mother and I got married. She knew about your mother. Knew I was going to marry your mother. Before she left Pittsburgh, I think I remember she told me she was pregnant. Maybe not. Heard afterward from her people she did have a baby. I never saw her after she moved away. And never laid eyes on the baby they said was mine. But I knew about him. Her brothers didn't particularly like me, but we all

knocked around together in those days, so I heard some
things about her and a baby. I'm sort of foggy on it now.
A long time ago, wasn't it. You're close to fifty yourself,
aren't you.

And he'd be older than I am. Right.

A little older, uh-huh.

What was the woman's name.

A Hankins when I knew her. Claudia. Claudia Hankins. Funny how your mind works. Name just popped.
Didn't know I still knew that name.

Something like a sigh or a long, drawn-out *uh-huh* or
just the rustle of my father's big body settling deeper into
itself on the seat beside me. We'd been riding awhile.
The previous day up before dawn to catch a Pittsburgh-
to-Charlotte, North Carolina, flight, a two-hundred-mile
drive to Greenwood, where we checked into a Holiday
Inn, then cruising the countryside with little stops here
and there—Abbeville Courthouse, Mount Zion churchyard—till dinnertime. My father was tired. Me too. My
eyes on the road looking for the Promiseland sign, but I
know his head's drooping. In a minute he'll be snoring.

My father always possessed the knack of falling asleep
instantly, no matter what was going on around him. Anywhere. Anytime. I remember being a kid and peeking up
from my mashed potatoes to catch his head slumping forward, the heavy lids of his eyes dropping shut. Or him
sprawled in the easy chair, oblivious of the slap of a Zane
Grey shoot-em-up he'd been reading when it hits the li-
noleum. My father, chin sunk in his black robe, snoozing
in the choir loft of Homewood A.M.E. Zion till the other
voices start up and his mouth opens to work a hymn with
his eyes still closed.

Maybe the trick of dozing off, absenting himself, had something to do with the late hours of so many years working as a waiter or his partying hard—drinking, gambling, chasing ladies—beginning after other people's parties ended. Never enough sleep so he stole snatches when he could.

Perhaps he was born tired or maybe my father stayed tired from the constant drubbing America laid on the heads of black men of his generation. Globe-traveling veterans of World War II the country needed to redomesticate. Maybe that's why my father and the other Negro men always wore those hats. Those stingy brims crimped just so, stetsons, jockey caps, tams, trilbies, baseball caps, derbies, berets, astrakhans, bowlers, straw boaters, all those stylized lids to contain themselves, express themselves, protect themselves from blows directed at their tender, nappy skulls.

Catnaps my father's way of calling time-out, perhaps. A break, when he could catch one, from the bloody battles he understood quite well he'd never win. Or maybe he's remembering all the distance and silence. Tuning out the world a minute, turning inward because there's no place else to go, as I find myself doing more and more at this age, like father like son, sinking, adrift in a space where you might try to sort things out, or ask who you are or forget or forgive. Or simply wondering sometimes if it makes any difference, this wondering, these differences, things changing, hurting, slipping away, you can neither find a place for in your mind or let go.

Anthony E. Cook

From Boys to Men: Breaking the Cycle of Pain for Our Sons

*Anthony Cook is a professor of law at the
Georgetown University Law Center. He writes
widely on critical legal studies, religion,
postmodernism, and cultural politics, and is the
author of a forthcoming collection of essays.*

Children come through us, not from us. The tension, turmoil, and torment that so often characterize parent-child relationships very often result from our failure as parents to acknowledge this truth. Our departure from it is sometimes conscious, but most often it is unconscious. Understandably, we desire to see our gene pools reincarnated through the miracle of birth: whose eyes does he have, whose mouth and nose do hers most resemble, whose drive, sensitivity, and idiosyncracies do they possess? We look for some tangible proof that through these creations we live on, that we have sustained the possibility of immortality, at least for another generation. Thus, we beam with pride at the suggestion that Junior is just "a chip off the old block," and that we can "spit out" the image of ourselves in another. Perhaps in this act of human creation, we become most like God. If so, herein lies our greatest danger and yet possibility.

The desire to kneel onto the shifting sands of human personality and mold our children into our image, breathing into them the thought patterns that will shape much of their conscious and unconscious behavior, often frustrates both parent and child and can cause more harm than good. When our molding and shaping is motivated by egotistical needs, and when we mistake our role as conduit for that of source, failing to acknowledge that these souls have merely traveled through us to this dimension, we lose the humility and love that only acceptance of our finiteness can bring.

In the humility engendered by the awareness of our limited understanding, we sometimes grasp the mysterious truth uttered by that prophet from Galilee who said in words that must have befuddled his listeners then as much as they confound us now: "Suffer the little children to come unto me; forbid them not; for of such is the Kingdom of God." Could it be that in our shaping and molding, our protecting and controlling, we distance ourselves and our children from the presence of God? Could it be that our children bear witness of our divine origin in ways that, through lens crafted by the values of this world, we no longer see? Could they be the gateways through which we adults might recover a joy, curiosity, hope, spontaneity, vulnerability, and inner paradise lost? Could we, through their stubborn insistence to wring as much life as they can from the moment, free from the pains of the past and the anxieties of the future, also be "born again"?

Humbled by the possibility that children have as much to teach us as we have to teach them, we are ready for the wonderful possibilities parenting can bring. Only then do we understand that our greatest task in parenting is not as molders and shapers of body and mind but as guides to our children's spiritual growth. Only then does parenting become infinitely more fulfilling, as we both guide and are guided by the light flowing through us into that new life that comes from God.

Kierkegaard observed, with typical irony, that "without God, I am too strong." In our failure to understand that children come through us and not from us, we risk being consumed by the power and control we exercise over that which we arrogantly claim to be our own. Unlike God in the Garden of Eden story, most of us lack the restraint necessary to mold, shape, give life to our creation, and then free it to choose what path it shall take. We want to hold on to and control our creations, whether those creations are thoughts, things, or human beings. The possession and control of that which is not ours to control is the true fall from grace, the alienation of man from God. Not even God desired to control His creation in such a way. Thus, He gave them the freedom to do that which He least desired them to do.

But when that soul which has manifested itself in this dimension as a newborn child is guided by, rather than molded by, parents who know its true origins, we become like God in a different and more liberating sense. No longer desiring to control our children, by shaping them into our image of what we think they should be, we create the necessary space for the unconditional love so vital to our journeys toward greater God consciousness. Thus, it is in this spiritual space of unconditional love that salvation truly lies for both parent and child.

As spiritual guides daring to love our children unconditionally, we know that the path we are traveling to spiritual awareness and wholeness is not the only path. From our finite perspective there can be no inherently better or worse, good or bad, right or wrong path. Indeed, we cannot say what the path taken has been until it is completed, and that only God can see. Who can say that paths which strike us as futile and totally wrong are not absolutely indispensable to the Creator's design? Faith is knowing that all paths lead back to God, for our soul belongs to its Creator, and thence must it ultimately return. The question is whether we will choose to travel our path with the conscious awareness and acceptance of the truth that we are but parts of God returning to God. As such, every experience, every event, and every expression of creation becomes an opportunity to know God more fully.

When we talk, as spiritually minded parents, of the path we have traveled and are traveling, it is not to demand that our children take a similar path or that they take the path we might or should have taken. It is to extract the lessons of spiritual growth and development we have learned and are learning along our way. It is to illuminate how experiences can give rise to greater intimacy with and acknowledgment of the infinite that transcends yet pervades our finite experience. We understand that every path has its own unique experiences. Those experiences, whether pleasant or unpleasant, have a place in our spiritual evolution when we see with spiritual eyes, listen with spiritual ears, and attune our souls to the call of the Divine.

Thus, children who have spiritual guides as parents follow their parents, not out of fear or custom but because, like moths in darkness, they are drawn to the light. They find in their parents' experiences and wisdom something their souls once knew but forgot, or something they should know but do not, or something they will know but do not yet. In this spiritual understanding of parenting, parents are liberated from the fear of losing control of their children, for they were never theirs to control from the start. Children are liberated from the fears of conditional love, those demons that destroy both body and soul. In this space void of fear, a true love takes hold that no poet or psalmist could treat justly. It is a love that passes all understanding and covers the multitude of faults, foibles, and failures to which the imperfect art of parenting gives rise.

The following narrative of my relationship with my father and its impact on my relationship with my children is a testimony of the redemptive value of unconditional love in parent/child relationships. Through this story I want to examine some of the ways in which this relationship often turns bitter and disharmonious. I also want to explore and understand the power of love to forgive and heal the pain that too often is recycled from one generation to the next.

A Narrative: Ending the Cycle of Pain

At the age of twenty-five, I lost both of my parents. Within six months my mother had died of heart disease and my father of cancer. Two and a half years later, my wife and I welcomed the first of our three boys into the world. My parents' deaths, combined with the birth of my first son, forced me to grapple with issues I was fully prepared to delay for yet a few more years. Suddenly not being able to call or visit my parents, particularly my mother, and seek their wisdom and counsel on matters pertaining to my still young marriage and growing family, I was forced to think deeply about the meanings of our relationships, about what it meant to be a parent and, particularly, a father to boys on the path to manhood.

My relationship with each parent was quite different, but as I now understand the spiritual journey I have been making, each was quite essential to my process of becoming. I want to explore what struck me then as a painful relationship with my father. I want to suggest how, in light of what I've said above, my experiences might be similar to many father-son relationships. Over the years I have concluded that my relationship with my father, as painful as it was at the time, has permitted me to forgive, heal, and love more fully, and for this I am eternally grateful that he, and no other, was my dad.

One observation I've made of parent-child relationships, which by no means holds true in all cases, is that father-son and mother-daughter relationships are more contentious and difficult than father-daughter or mother-son relationships. The reason, I believe, has to do with the standards of manhood that fathers often use to judge, unconsciously many times, their sons and the standards of womanhood by which mothers judge their daughters. This issue is a particularly troubling one for a historically oppressed people like black Americans who, precisely because black manhood and black womanhood have been deemed by the larger society as a contradiction of terms, often feel too unloved to love and who, from that void of self-contempt, abuse the power of judgment in hopes of affirming their own self-worth.

Let me explain. Young children made to feel unworthy, made to feel that they constantly miss the elusive and ever changing mark of manhood or womanhood, generally respond in one of two ways. Either they accept the standard they are presented and feel unworthy and ashamed when they consistently fail to satisfy the standard, or they reject the standard and internalize the anger that results from being forced to reject, even kill, that with which they would prefer to be in harmony. The problem is worsened when one realizes that because the standard and the standard bearer are often indistinguishable, it becomes necessary to reject or kill the standard bearer as well. When the standard bearer is a mother or father, the implications are clear. The child is forced either to commit spiritual suicide or spiritual patricide.

As a child I committed spiritual patricide as a defense against the degradation of my self-worth, as a defense against what I felt to be the only alternative to spiritual suicide. The resentment and anger that developed from feeling forced to spiritually kill that with which I desired harmony would haunt me for many years.

Now, it is important to understand that the victim of our spiritual murder need not be a villain. Indeed, the more admirable the victim is in other respects, the more intense are our feelings of resentment and anger at having to spiritually kill them. Such was the case with my father. He was not an evil man. He physically spanked me only once in my childhood. I never saw him raise a hand of abuse to my mother. I never saw him drink, sleep around, or abuse others. He was a responsible worker who always went beyond the call of duty, who always brought his check home to his family and was a model neighbor and deacon of the church. He had a great sense of humor when he desired, and on many occasions I noted the effects of his irresistible charm upon even the coldest of women who, after a few minutes in his presence, would be giddy with delight. He built our home with his own hands and possessed expertise in an astonishing array of things, from carpentry, plumbing, and electrical work to car repair and farming.

My father was strong, smart, and talented. He managed to do more with a third-grade education than I have seen most do with Ph.D.'s. Why wouldn't anyone want to be like him? Of course I did. But his talents, gifts, interests, and opportunities were not my own. I had come through him, but not from him. Neither he nor I had evolved to the point that we understood the difference and felt at ease enough to accept it. So what might have been a different relationship was, perhaps, the relationship it had to be to get his soul and mine to the space of spiritual awareness they are now and will be in the life to come. Thus, I have come to have no regrets.

But from my more limited perspective as a child and as a young adult, the problem was that for most of my childhood I rarely felt loved by this man I called Daddy. Too young to know or understand the circumstances and conditions that had shaped his life and personality, all I could see was his meanness and disdain. I could not forgive the many ways he made my mother cry with his harsh words, without raising or even threatening to raise his hand. I still remember running, both as a child and teenager, to comfort and beg her to stop crying. I could not forgive the way nothing I ever did was good enough for him, how I never heard him say he loved me or was proud of me and heard only his customary litany of putdowns: "lazy," "trifling," not worth a "hill of beans," "go on in the house with the women folk." I would gladly have taken a hundred beatings to escape the scars his words left on my spirit.

In my heart, then, I had to kill him, him and the stultifying standards of manhood by which he judged me unworthy. As a boy coming into manhood, I wanted and needed the approval of this man who seemed bigger than life, whose strength, courage, and skill I always felt obliged to strive for but never felt I could attain. So I killed him in my spirit. He became the man who conceived me and nothing more. He became a biological link, a genetic repository, but void of emotional or psychological significance for my life.

I defined myself against the standards by which he judged me, in quiet defiance of him. If growing and plaiting long hair in the seventies irritated him, I would braid it in his presence. If I could not work a hammer and saw with the dexterity befitting true men, I would read books as he labored mightily beneath his car. If being able to support a family economically from the sweat of one's brow was so important to him, I would work some school nights, every weekend, and all summer to prove myself a better man than him. I would tell no one of my secret sin, but in a thousand ways I would reveal my deed to him—praising my mother to others in his presence for accomplishments that he might surely want credit, showing warmth and affection to her and coldness to him, bestowing what gifts and pleasures I could at such an age on her while again slighting him, disagreeing for the sake of disagreeing and on and on. . . .

But spiritual murder is never as easy as it seems. Our bruised and pained egos convince us that the deed will soothe our tortured souls. But it is not our soul that is in need of healing. Rather, it is the unconditional love that is our soul that stands ready to heal. Since the soul of God knows no vengeance, pain, lack, hatred, or death, it can never be satisfied by these things. It knows and thus can only desire unity, balance, and harmony. Thus, as I defied my father and defined myself and manhood over and against him, I still felt empty. My quiet revenge was not as sweet as I hoped it would be. The ego, my lower self, cried for more blood, convincing me that the hole I thought was in my soul, the pain that only really my ego's heart experienced, might eventually be pacified by greater slaughter still. So I concealed my pain with an armor and shield made of words and smiles, charm and finesse, and quietly turned the sword of my embattled heart toward others. I allowed them to come but so close to my pain, and if they dared to transgress my sover-eignty, I spiritually killed them too, threatening as they did to expose my pain and shame.

So here was the sad irony. The more I tried not to be him, to defy and seek revenge against him, the more I became him. I became a master of words, capable at once of taking you to heights of ecstasy and then to the depths of sorrow. The thing I perhaps most detested about him, his verbal abuse of my mother, I was now able to do, and did with the greatest of ease, to other women. Having been abused in some ways, I became an abuser in those very ways. Had certain things in my life happened dif-ferently, I have no doubt I would be reproducing with my sons the same cycle of abuse from which I now know my father was himself seeking escape.

To be sure, the standards of manhood I would impose would be different, reflecting my particular set of truths, talents, skills, and interests. But the game would be the same. Failing to understand that they are essences of God passing through me and not collections of genes coming from me, I would seek to mold, shape, and judge rather than guide, illuminate, and love. My father's pain became my pain with a different face and would transform yet again to be my boys' pain if the chain of bondage remained unbroken. On them I would impose standards that, in my eyes, they could never satisfy. My wounded ego would, most times, convince me that the route to manhood was the harsh control and judgment of others, particularly those, like a son, whose shortcomings would serve to convince me that at least I was more a man than he.

What, then, began to break for me this cycle of pain? In short, it was love. Love and the wisdom that only experience and a prayerful spirit can bring allowed me to resurrect my father from the spiritual grave into which my heart had cast him. Resurrection was made possible by three things. The first was that while my relationship with my father often felt tormented, alienated, and conditional, I did know unconditional love. Through my mother I had beheld its awe-inspiring beauty, basked in the joyful radiance of its light, and felt through every fiber of my being its healing power. In her presence I felt protected, loved, and nourished. I always felt that no matter what I did or became in life, from prince to pauper, her love would be unchanging. The blessed assurance that this one thought has brought to my life is more than I have either understanding or talent to write.

With a spirituality that transcended religion, whose breath and depth I am still trying to fathom, she had long uncovered the deed I thought was buried from view in my heart. Even through her tears, as I cried trying to console her, she would hold me and try to explain why I should not do what she feared I might. How could she say that she loved a man who would say such cruel things, disparaging her color, weight, intelligence, and service to all? It was too much for a young mind to understand. But yet she loved him. And let there be no mistake. This was not fear but love. I never saw bitterness. I never saw resentment. I never saw any of the emotions that tormented my soul. She loved him. Why? Because she was able to see through his personality to the purity and perfection of his soul. While at times he might have forgotten, as do we all, who he was, she could look at him and see God.

The second set of experiences that helped me to break out of the cycle of pain was the prolonged exposure to my oldest sister's husband. I had no brothers, and by the time I entered the first grade, I was the only child of my parents' four children remaining at home. My brother-in-law modeled for me a different conception of manhood that I remember studying and evaluating but not realizing how much I needed until later. Through him I began to see that men/husbands/fathers could be simultaneously strong, kind, even-tempered, and responsible. I never witnessed him utter a harsh word to my sister. I saw a comfort level that his children had around him that I could only dream of having with my father.

He seemed to work more and better with words, papers, books, and ideas than with saws and hammers, and this helped me to see that my talents and interests were not strange. Growing up in the sixties and seventies in a small town like Magnolia, Mississippi, I didn't have much prolonged exposure to people who worked primarily with their minds and words. Teachers and preachers pretty much exhausted the field. I became both, and my brother-in-law's example helped me with what would become a pervasive sense of guilt from which it took me many years to recover, given my thoroughly working-class and rural background. This was the guilt of feeling that thinking, writing, and speaking, pursuing a life of the mind, being an intellectual, was not really work and therefore I was not really a man.

But the most important thing my relationship with my brother-in-law accomplished was a sense of self-affirmation as a young man. Like my mother, he always asked my opinion of things. He wanted to know how I felt about things. He really thought, or knew that it was important for me to believe he thought, that I actually had something worthwhile and important to say. Given the feelings I was going through with my father, the sense of self-doubt beginning to pervade my thoughts, I needed a man such as this in my life. The one thing my mother could not heal, my fear that I could not be a man, he helped me, over countless weekends that I worked in his yard and stayed the night, played ball, watched television, and just talked, to overcome.

The third set of experiences involved my father. By my senior year in high school, it seemed clear that whatever alternative path I had carved out held tremendous promise. I was senior class president, slated to be the valedictorian of my class. I held the highest cumulative average over three years of biology, chemistry, and physics, had won numerous prizes throughout the state in forensics and debate, while working fifteen to twenty hours a week at local restaurants, and was accepted by Princeton University for admission in the fall of 1978. Although I still had never heard the words of encouragement or pride I so desperately thought I needed from my father, I did overhear one of his conversations that complicated my understanding of his character.

He was talking one afternoon with one of the many community folk who would stop by our house—situated at the crossroads of the community, across from the church. As I walked through the house to the front porch, I could hear him talking about me. But this time they were new words, with a different melody and cadence, and they both moved and confused me. He was actually bragging to someone about me. I could hardly believe my ears. "My boy" did this, he would say. "My boy" won this, he went on. He encouraged the visitor, who I could tell was growing tired of his bragging, to go into the house and look at all my trophies and awards. I did not understand this. He had complained so about all the practices and trips that had made those awards possible. He had, on more than one occasion, suggested that my love of drama, poetry, and oratory was "sissy stuff." How could he now be proud of me? Did he have a right to be proud? Was he sincere or just jumping on the bandwagon of my success? I was at once ecstatic that I was now hearing the first utterances of his approval and angry that it was coming so late, and still not directly to me. Yet on another occasion his sincerity seemed even more unquestionable.

Early one Saturday evening, my mother and I had gone to church. She had forgotten her glasses and asked me to run home and get them. I was walking around to the back door of our house when I heard the sound of my father praying. This was somewhat odd, because while I had often seen my mother praying throughout the day, it was not customary to see my father do so this early in the evening. As I listened to him through the raised window, his words shook my heart. He was actually praying for me. By name he was praying for me. He was thanking God for having blessed me in the things I had done. He was asking God to watch over me as I traveled so far away from home. As strange as it seems, I had never thought my daddy prayed for me, that he cared enough, loved enough. . . . So the sincerity of his words shook me, and all of a sudden I didn't know what or how to feel.

But it was the third incident that year that most changed my consciousness about him. He had incessantly counseled me not to drive the car through a certain intersection in town that was particularly busy, but instead always to take an alternate route. Through the lens of my pain and the cynicism it engendered, I could interpret this only as yet another put-down on my ability and his ultimate distrust of my judgment and worth. So I transgressed his law deliberately, as I tried to do whenever it was possible without hurting, embarrassing, or bringing shame to my mother. As I turned through the intersection this day, my mind was elsewhere, and before I knew it, police lights and onlookers were crowded all around. I had turned in front of another car that had the right of way. But this was not just any car—it was a brand new, custom-ordered, black on black Monte Carlo belonging to the daughter of the judge of Pike County. She was furious, and I was frightened to the brink of death.

When my father arrived with my sister, I expected the worst: public scorn added to humiliation, a public lashing, who knew? Whatever the punishment, I certainly felt I deserved it and more. I was ashamed, feeling every bit as naked as the mythical characters Adam and Eve, aware of the separation from God their choice had wrought. As he walked toward me, I could not see his eyes, for my head was bent low by the weight of shame. To my amazement, without really looking at the car, his first words were "Are you all right?" I choked with relief, so shocked was I that he was not angry. When I did look into his eyes, I saw no anger, frustration, or embarrassment. I saw only his concern for me, his son. Never did he mention the incident to me. Never did he say, "I told you so," or chide me for transgressing his law. There was only mercy and, yes, for the first time I saw it, unconditional love.

It would be nice to tell you that all of this had a fairy-tale ending, that this moment totally transformed my experiences with my father, that we began to talk and, on occasion, even told each other of our mutual respect and love. But reality is more complicated than fairy tales, and so was our relationship. When you combine the love of my mother, the role modeling of my brother-in-law, and these three major experiences that gave me deeper insight into the soul of my father, I had begun to desire, by the time I left my hometown, to forgive him and, more important, to forgive myself as well. It took longer than that for me actually to forgive and even longer still for me to start consciously undoing some of the negative behavior to which my anger had unconsciously given rise. But now at least I wanted to forgive, and that was the crucial step. To be sure, I see residues still. But having moved beyond blaming myself or him, I know they too will someday succumb to the unconditional love I now feel more and more every day.

My studies at Princeton, along with the experiences that only time could bring, gave me greater insight into the historical, sociological, and psychological context that had shaped so much of what my father was and was not. In history I learned things about the racist world of my father's generation. In sociology I learned of dysfunctions within social units, like the family, that arise from institutions of domination and exploitation like slavery and segregation. In psychology I learned how these dysfunctions often produce certain personality quirks and disorders of which the person is almost always unaware. In short, I started to assemble the theoretical apparatus that allowed me to come to grips with so many things that troubled my childhood and would, in a different guise, plague my adulthood.

In numerous conversations with my mother, family, and even my father, I began to ask questions that allowed me to construct a narrative about his life and how his experiences must have made him feel and how his responses to those feelings must have often seemed beyond his control. Here was a man born in 1910, who witnessed the world transform right before his eyes. As a kid, most people traveled by horse and buggy or by foot. By the time I was born, a car-filled interstate and a jet-streaked sky were common occurrences. Society had moved from radio and mail as the primary means of communication to television, phone, and computer chips that conveyed information in billionths of a second. He had seen the decline of agrarian, the rise of industrial, the decline of industrial and the rise of informational economies all in one lifetime. He experienced the great exodus of black people from rural to urban and South to North and the concomitant dislocation these shifts wrought on home and community. The world had changed more rapidly over his lifetime than it had over the past two thousand years.

Many of those changes undoubtedly impacted his childhood life, fostering economic uncertainty, family instability, and emotional fragility. He left home at thirteen because of an abusive relationship between his stepfather and his mother in which he became embroiled. His biological father was never married to his mother, and feeling neither a part of his biological father's family nor welcomed in his stepfather's family, he probably felt a degree of abandonment that few of us know.

The yoke of racism in Mississippi was not an easy burden to bear in the years of his youth. I later heard the stories of rape, lynching, and terror that characterized much of his life. As a very young child I remember hearing my father refer to white girls in stores on which he depended for short-term credit—girls younger than any of his own daughters—as Ma'am and Miss as they disrespectfully called him by his first name. It enraged me even then, although I didn't know why. God only knows what, over the years, it must have done to him.

He knew more about the dark side of Mississippi than I could ever know at that age, having been born as late as 1960. So when he refused to let me date girls from the nearby town of Tylertown, it was not out of mean-spiritedness. He simply remembered their Klan meetings, the night riders, and the horrors that undoubtedly befell friends of his youth who dared to be caught there after dark. I now understand that much of the rigidity I experienced as arbitrary was coming out of a set of experiences, terrifying experiences, that shaped his understanding of the world he had endured and that his children would have to inhabit. Understandably, his impulse was to protect, and in the countryside of Mississippi at night, the most protected place a black man could be was in his own community, around his own people. And sometimes even that was not enough.

It would have helped had he explained the context, motivations, and purposes of his dictates more. But perhaps this was to expect too much. The experiences that gave rise to the fear and anger he possessed were, I imagine, too terrifying and painful to retrieve. Having spent too many days, like the tormented character Sethe in Toni Morrison's *Beloved*, beating back the past, he chose to forget why or how he had come to feel as he did. Life shows me more and more why many choose this way of coping. But the method is as dangerous as it is understandable, for it is the central link in the cycle of pain and chain of bondage we reproduce from one generation to the next.

Conclusion

It was the touch of unconditional love that opened my eyes to my father's pain, that made me want to know his story and heal the source of our mutual grief. Through that love I resurrected him from the spiritual grave in which my ego had buried him. In his resurrected state I saw with spiritual eyes what my mother had seen through her tears—*a precious soul struggling to be free from the pain of the past, the pressure of the present, and the fear of the future.*

At this writing, my boys are only seven, four, and two. Most of the time I have no idea if I'm doing the best thing for them. I do know this, however. When I most understand the reality that they have come through me and not from me, my whole orientation toward them and toward parenting shifts. I behold them as wonders in and of themselves, on a spiritual journey that will be the journey they and they alone must make. My role as guide is not to mold and shape them, for their Creator has done that from the beginning of time. It is to remind them of who they are and why they are here until they see it more fully themselves. And the great part of the reminding, I now believe, comes not from the conventional forms of morality, convention, and dogmatic preachings that characterized my youth. It comes instead from their attraction to the light that I emanate as a father also on a spiritual journey toward oneness with God.

That journey creates its own morality, one that transcends the legalistic prohibitions that characterize so much of our religious habits and theories of parenting. Central to it is an understanding that my higher Self, my spiritual Self, the Self that is of God, is unconditional love, and that this higher Self belongs to a Kingdom not of this world but to a Kingdom found only in the innermost recesses of my Soul. And when I have not forgotten who I am, this unconditional love, which the Self so naturally is, emanates and illuminates the paths my children will take. I don't desire so much to control the path they take as much as to illuminate their way. So if ever they get lost in the darkness of their egos, the paths filled with pain, self-hate, and destruction, they will eventually look up and see the light of unconditional love and, in moving toward that light, rediscover the light within themselves.

Recently, my oldest son's class created Father's Day cards for their fathers. One of the statements the teacher asked the students to complete was: "I love Dad best when . . ." My son wrote, "when he smiles at me and it makes me smile back." Of all the things he could have written about buying toys, playing basketball, reading books, going to the movies, etc., he chose something as simple and yet as spiritually profound as a smile. To think that so much can be communicated through a smile is a humbling thought for a parent. Because when the rules, punishment, and fabulous theories of parenting have passed, it is in that quiet space where Spirit speaks to Spirit in its own language of Unconditional Love that true parenting takes place.

I understood my son perfectly. His words brought tears to my eyes. But this time it was not because I thought about all the times I needed, but didn't get, a smile from my father that could "make me smile back." It was because I knew I was breaking the cycle of pain for my sons. I knew healing had begun.

Cornel West

On Black Fathering

Cornel West is a professor of Afro-American studies and religion at Harvard University. He is the author of the bestselling book Race Matters, *as well as* Keeping Faith *and* Prophesy Deliverance! *He lectures widely on topics ranging from philosophy to democracy and contemporary race issues.*

One of the most difficult tasks to accomplish in American society is to be a solid, caring, and loving black father. To be a good black father, first you have to negotiate all of the absurd attacks and assaults on your humanity and on your capacity and status as a human being. Second, you have to provide materially and economically, as well as nurture psychologically, personally, and existentially. All of this requires a deep level of maturity. By maturity I mean a solid understanding of who one is as a person, and a sense of sacrifice and courage. For black men to reach that level of maturity and understanding is almost miraculous given the dehumanizing context for black men, and yet millions and millions have done it. It is a tribute to fulfill the highest standards of fatherhood. When I think of my own particular case, I think of my father, my grandfather, and his father, because what they were able to do was to sustain some sense of dignity and sacrifice even as they dealt with all the arrows that were coming at them on every level in American society.

Let's consider the economic level. In America, generally speaking, patriarchal definitions of men in relation to the economic front means you have a job and provide for your family. Many black men did not (and do not) make enough money to provide for their families adequately because of their exclusion from jobs with a living wage. They then oftentimes tended, and tend, to accent certain patriarchal identities (e.g., predatory or abusive behavior) in lieu of the fact that they could not perform the traditional patriarchal roles in American society.

Then on the home front, where black men had and have, oftentimes, wives who were and are subject to such white supremacist abuse, either at the white home where these sisters work(ed) or as a service worker in other parts of white society, most black men had to deal with the kinds of scars and bruises that come from knowing that you were supposed to protect your woman, as it were, which is also part of the patriarchal identity in America—a man ought to be able to protect his woman but could not protect her from the vicious abuse. Many black men also recognized that there was a relation between their not being able to get a job given the discrimination and segregation on the one hand and the tremendous power wielded by those white men who were often condoning the abuse of their own wives.

How children perceive their father is another interesting component of the dynamic that black fathers have to negotiate. How are black fathers able to convey to their children some affirmative sense of self, some sense of reality—given what is happening to these men on the economic front, given what many of them know is happening to their wives outside of the house, and given the perception by their own children that they are unable to fulfill the expected patriarchal role? In the tradition of the

black father, the best ones—I think my grandfather and
dad are good examples—came up with ways of negotiating a balance so that they would recognize that exclusion from the economic sphere was real, and recognize
that possible abuse of their wives was real, and also recognize that they had to sustain a connection with their
kids in which their kids could see the best in them despite the limited and dehumanizing circumstances under
which they functioned.

My mother happened to be a woman who was not
abused in the fashion described above. I remember one
incident when a white policeman disrespected my
mother. Dad went at him verbally and, in the eyes of the
police, ended up violating the law. At that point he just
drew a line in the sand that said, "You're going too far."
I thank God that a number of incidents like that didn't
happen, or he would have ended up in jail forever—like
so many other brothers who just do not allow certain levels of disrespect of their mother, wife, sister, or daughter.
As a man, what I was able to see in Dad was his ability
to transform his own pain with a sense of laughter, and
a sense of empathy, and a sense of compassion for others.
This was a real act of moral genius Dad accomplished,
and I think that it is part of the best of a tradition of moral
genius. Unfortunately, large numbers of black men do not
reach that level because the rage and the anger is just too
deep; it just burns them out and consumes their soul. Fortunately, on the other hand, you do have many black men
that achieve this level and some that go beyond it.

In my own case as a father, I certainly tried to emulate
and imitate Dad's very ingenious ways of negotiating the
balances between what was happening on these different

fronts, but because of the sacrifices he and Mom made, I had access to opportunities that he did not. When my son Cliff was born, I was convinced that I wanted to try to do for him what Dad had done for me. But it was not to be—there was no way that I could be the father to my son that my dad was to me. Part of it was that my circumstances were very different. Another part was simply that I was not the man that my father was. My brother is actually the shining example of building on the rich legacy of my dad as a father much more than I am, because he gives everything—right across the board. He is there —whatever the circumstance—has spent time with the kids; he is always there in the same way that Dad was there for us. I'll always try to be a rich footnote to my brother, yet as a father I have certainly not been the person that he was. The effort has been there, the endeavor too, but the circumstances (as well as my not being as deep a person as he or my father), have not enabled me to measure up. On the other hand, my son Cliff turned out to be a decent and fascinating person—and he is still in process, of course.

The bottom line for my dad was always love, and he was a deeply Christian man—his favorite song was "I Will Trust in the Lord." He had a profound trust. His trust was much more profound than mine in some ways, even though I work at it. He had a deep love, and that's the thing I've tried to build on with Cliff. My hope and my inclination is that Cliff feels this love, but certainly it takes more than love to nurture and father a son or a daughter.

The most important things for black fathers to try to do is to give of themselves, to try to exemplify in their own behavior what they want to see in their sons and daughters, and, most important, to spend time with and give attention to their children. This is a big challenge, yet it is critical as we move into the twenty-first century.

The most difficult task of my life was to give the eulogy for my father. Everything else pales in the face of this challenge. Hence what Dad means to me—like my family, Cliff and Elleni—constitutes who and what I am and will be.

Eulogy

Clifton Lincoln West, Jr. What a man. What an individual. What a person. What a servant. We gather here this afternoon in this sacred place and this consecrated space to say good-bye. To bid farewell to a good man, a great Christian who lived a grand and loving life. When I think of my father, I cannot but think of what he said to that reporter from the *Sacramento Bee* when they asked him, "What is it about you and what is it about your family—do you have a secret?" Dad said, "No, we live by Grace—in addition to that, me and his mother, we try to *be there*." I shall never forget that my father was not simply a man of quiet dignity, steadfast integrity, and high intelligence, but fundamentally and quintessentially he was a man of love, and love means being there for others. That's why when I think of Dad I recall that precious moment in the fifteenth chapter of John in the eleventh and twelfth verse: "These things have I given unto you that my joy might remain in you, and that your joy might be full. This is my commandment that ye love one another as I have loved you."

In the midst of Dad's sophistication and refinement he was always for real. He was someone who was down-to-earth because he took this commandment seriously, and it meant he had to cut against the grain in a world in which he was going to endure lovingly and with compassion. Isn't that what the very core of the gospel is about? The thirteenth chapter of I Corinthians—that great litany of love that Dr. King talked about—deals with it. Dad used to read it all the time. I will never forget when he took me to college in Cambridge, the first time I ever flew on an airplane (it cost about ninety-five dollars then). Dad told me, "Corn, we're praying for you, and always remember: 'Though I speak with the tongues of men and of angels and have not love, I become as a sounding brass or a tinkling cymbal. And though I have the gift of prophecy, and understand all mysteries, and all knowledge; and though I have all faith, so that I could remove mountains, and have not love, I am nothing.' "

As we stand here on these stormy banks of Jordan and watch Dad's ship go by, may I remind each and every one of you that we come from a loving family, a courageous people of African descent, and a rich Christian tradition. We have seen situations in which history has pushed our backs against the wall, and life has knocked us to our knees. In the face of despair and degradation sometimes we know that all we can do is sing a song, or crack a smile, or say a prayer. Yet we refuse to allow grief and misery to have the last word.

Dad was a man of love, and if I was to adopt his perspective at this very moment, he would say "Corn, don't push me in the limelight, keep your mother in mind, don't focus on me, keep the family in mind—I'm just a servant passing through." That's the kind of father I had. But he didn't come to it by himself, you see. He was part of a family, he was part of a people, he was part of a tradition that went all the way back to gut-bucket Jim Crow Louisiana, September 7, 1928. He was not supposed to make it, you see. Nobody would have believed that Clifton Lincoln West, Jr., the third child of C. L. West and Lovey West, would have been able to aspire to the heights that he did. No one would have predicted or projected that he would make it through the first three months in Louisiana—Cliff was not supposed to make that trip, you know. He was born the year before the stock market crashed. His family stayed three months in Louisiana, and Grandfather and Grandmother, with three young children in a snowstorm, journeyed on a train to Tulsa, Oklahoma. You all know what Tulsa, Oklahoma, was like. It was seven years after the major riot in this country in which over three hundred folks—black folks —were killed and Greenwood, Archer and Pine—that GAP corner—the Wall Street of black America was all burned out. But Grandmama had something else in mind, and the Lord did too.

Dad went on to Paul Laurence Dunbar Elementary School—to give you an idea of what side of town they were living on—and George Washington Carver Junior High School, and Booker T. Washington High School. It was there that he got to choose the idea of pulling from the best of the world but remaining not of the world. I like that about Dad. He wasn't so excessively pious or so excessively rigid that he became naive and got caught up in narrow doctrines and creeds and thought he was better than anybody else. That's not the kind of man he was.

No. His faith was grounded in a love because he knew that he had fallen short of the glory of God. He knew he had inadequacies and shortcomings, but he was going to struggle anyhow; he was going to keep keeping on anyway.

After high school he went on to the military for three years. He could have easily given his life for this country. When he returned to Tulsa, Oklahoma, he was refused admission at the University of Tulsa, and then went on to that grand institution, Fisk University, where he met that indescribably wonderful, beautiful, lovable honor student from Orange, Texas—Irene Bias. I'll never forget when we were at Fisk together, he described the place right outside Jubilee Hall where they met. I said, "Dad, that's a special place," and he said, "Yes, that meeting was the beginning of the peak of my life." As their love began to grow and multiply, the army grabbed him back again for eighteen months, but in the years to come they had young Clifton, my brother, to whom I'm just a footnote; myself, of course; and Cynthia and Cheryl. We moved from Oklahoma through Topeka, Kansas, on our way to 8008 48th Avenue, Glen Elder. Yes, how proud we were driving up in that bright orange Mercury. We were at the cutting edge of residential breakdown in Sacramento, but along the way, for almost a decade, Dad, and the men of Glen Elder—Mr. Peters, Mr. Pool, Mr. Powell, Mr. Reed—these were black men who cared and who worked together. These overworked yet noble men built the little league diamond by themselves, and then they organized the league into ten teams—minor and major leagues for the neighborhood. They provided a means by which character and integrity could be shaped among

the young brothers. Then every Sunday, onto Shiloh—
"can't wait for the next sermon of Reverend Willie P.
Cooke, just hope that he didn't go too long"—but we
knew that the Lord was working in him. Dad would always tell us, "You know how blessed I am, how blessed
we are. Never think that we've come as far as we have
on our own."

When we were in trouble, there was Mr. Fields, Mrs.
Ray, and Mrs. Harris—there were hundreds of folks who
made a difference. You all remember when Dad went to
the hospital when he was thirty-one years old and the
doctors had given up on him. There was a great sadness
on Forty-eighth Avenue because he had left Mom with
four little children. Granddad—the Reverend C. L. West,
left his church for months to come and be with Mom—
Grandmom came as well—and Dad was in the hospital
in Oakland. They had given up on him; the medical profession had reached its conclusion and said they could do
nothing. And we said, "We know the power. Let Him
step in." We knew that Reverend Cook hadn't been
preaching that "Jesus is a rock in a weary land, and water
in dry places, and food when you are hungry, and a mind
regulator and a heart fixer" for nothing. And we came to
Calvary in prayer.

Can you imagine how different our lives would have
been if we had lost Dad then, in 1961, rather than 1994?
Even in the midst of our fear we rejoice. It would have
been a different world for each and every one of us, especially the children. Dad kept going after his recovery.
He worked at McClellan Air Force Base—steadily missed
some of those promotions he should have got, but he

stayed convinced that he was going to teach people right no matter what, even given his own situation.

That's another thing I loved about him. People always ask me, "West, why do you still talk about love? It's played out. Why when you talk about blackness is it always linked to white brothers and sisters and yellow brothers and sisters and red brothers and sisters and brown brothers and sisters?" And I tell them about John 15:11–12. I tell them that I dedicated my life a long time ago to the same Jesus that Dad dedicated his life to, to the same Jesus that Reverend C. L. West dedicated his life, to the same Jesus that my grandfather on my mother's side and my grandmother on my mother's side dedicated their lives to, but, more important, I saw in the concrete, with Dad and Mom, a love that transcends skin pigmentation. I saw it on the ground. Dad taught us that even as you keep track of the injustice, you don't lose track of the humanity. That's what love and being there is all about. Dad made it a priority and preference to be there for us. He made a choice. It meant that he would live a life of interruptions because those who are fundamentally committed to being there are going to be continually interrupted—your own agenda, your own project, is going to be interfered with. Dad was always open to that kind of interruption. He was able to translate a kind of unpredictable interruption into a supportive intervention in somebody else's life. More important, Dad realized that a being-there kind of love meant that you had to have follow up and follow through. One could not just show up—one has to follow up and follow through. This is the most difficult aspect of it. Love is inseparable from pain and hurt and sadness and sorrow and disappointment, but Dad knew that you had to have follow up and follow through. He knew that you had to struggle in the midst of that pain and that hurt—you had to have just not simply the high moments of love, but the funk of love, the stink and the stench of love. In all of his relationships Dad embodied precisely that struggle with the high moments of love and the low moments of love. He knew that the cross was not just about smiles and that it was not just about celebration—it was about sadness, stench, and funk. That is what the blood was about, not Kool-aid but blood. That's how inseparable scars, bruises, and wounds are from joy, affirmation, and wholeness. If you were serious about love, if you were serious about being there for people you were going to be there in the midst of any situation, any circumstances, any condition. Dad realized that God being there for us in any situation and circumstance meant that if he was going to be God-like, he had to be there in any situation for us. I've been alive now for forty years, and on Thursday I'll be forty-one years old, and *not once has my mother or father disappointed me.* They have always been there. That is a blessing, and I do not deserve it. It's a blessing, and I am thankful for it.

So as we bid farewell to Dad, I want you all to know that I am looking forward to a family reunion. I am looking forward to union together on the other side of the Jordan. I am looking forward to seeing Dad in a place where the wicked will cease their troubling and the weary shall be at rest. I tell you when I get there, I'm going down Revelation Boulevard to the corner of John Street, right around the corner from Mark's place. But I want to go to Nahum's place. I don't want to be in Jeremiah's house, it would be too crowded. I don't even want to be down on Peter Street, too many people there—I want some quiet time. I want to sit down with C. L. West, I want to sit down with Nick Bias, and I want to sit down with Aunt Juanita, and I want to sit down with Aunt Tiny. And I want to sit down with Dad! I want to let them know that we did the best that we could to keep alive the best of the legacy of love that they left to us. And when we come together, we will come together in a way in which there will be no more tears, no more heartache, no more heartbreak, no more sadness and sorrow, no more agony and anguish. We shall sit at the feet of the Lord and be blessed, and our souls will look back and wonder how we got over, how we got over.

Martin Kilson

Notes on Black Parenting in the Late Twentieth Century

Martin Kilson is the Frank G. Thompson Professor of Government at Harvard. He is the author of many books, including Political Change in a West African State, Key Issues in the Afro-American Experience, *and* The African Diaspora. *He has lectured worldwide on politics, Africa, and the academy.*

Some Context

First and foremost, it is important to underline that it is the late twentieth century, not the early twentieth century, in which our discussion of black parenting is taking place. Why emphasize at the outset this period distinction? Because family culture in American life has changed fundamentally during the four generations between 1900 and 1995. For American family patterns as a whole, we need do no more than note the divorce rate for the average American family as of the 1990s—a rate just about at the fifty percent range of all marriages. And if we had solid data on that broader and more elusive index of family instability called the separation rate—the rate of divided marriages but not yet legalized—the index of family instability in American life is even greater.

Some sixty years ago—in the 1930s—the character of family culture also exhibited weaknesses, but on a lower level than in our era. If we use the broad index of family instability Gunnar Myrdal and his colleagues wrote about in their classic study of African-American life fifty years ago called *An American Dilemma: The Negro Problem and Modern Democracy*, namely, "broken families," data in

Table I reveal that while there was clearly family instability for all American families regardless of race, its rate
was significantly below the pattern in the 1990s. Data in
this table also show that sixty years ago the "broken family" rate among blacks was ten percentage points greater
than among whites. And another set of data in the Myrdal study show that unwed births were another feature
of weakness in family culture among blacks some sixty
years ago—a weakness that occurred eight times more
frequently than among native-born whites. In the 1990s,
while some two-thirds of black births are to unwed mothers, nearly one-fifth of white births are to unwed mothers,
and just over two-thirds of black family households are
female-headed households.

Another important contextual dynamic to note when
discussing black parenting issues in our era is the overall
profile of the black American social structure. When
America entered World War II in 1941, some 90 percent
of black Americans were either weak working-class or
poor, with the remainder being equally divided between
stable working-class and middle-class. By the middle
1980s, a veritable revolution had occurred. Today, some
60 percent of black households fall into what might be
called the "mobile strata" social category, which breaks
down into some 45 percent of black households located
as middle-class and some 15 percent ranked as upper-
class households. In family income attributes related to
the new black "mobile strata," out of a total of 10,488,000
black households in 1990, some 246,000 earned between
$50,000 and $55,000 annually; some 92,000 black households earned more than $70,000 annually; some 8,000
earned more than $100,000 annually; and generally for

two-parent black families by 1990 (35 percent of all black families) they earned on average $85 for every $100 earned on average by white families. Another dimension of the new black "mobile strata" can be seen from data on the new range of professional jobs that blacks have entered during the period from mid-1960s to mid-1990s. By 1990, some 2.1 percent of 630,000 marketing and public relations managers were black; 6.3 percent of 302,000 property and real estate managers were black; 6.7 percent of 882,000 computer programmers were black; 15.5 percent of 192,000 educational and vocational counselors; 7.6 percent of 1,325,000 accountants and auditors; 7.1 percent of 2,494,000 registered nurses; 7.2 percent of 479,000 therapists (occupational-physical); 7.2 percent of 1,640,000 engineering technicians; 2 percent of 83,000 biological scientists; 24 percent of master sergeants and 31 percent of sergeant major ranks in the armed forces; and, finally, also in armed forces, some 12.5 percent of majors, 12.4 percent of captains, and 11.5 percent of lieutenants are black.

Of course, with this major transformation has also been a persistent large minority of black households trapped in the "static strata"—that is, weak working-class and poor households. Some 40 percent of black households fall into this category. And within this is a hyper-poor group of people popularly called the black underclass— a sector that has high levels of crime and black-on-black violence, and is riddled with sundry social disorders like poor education achievement, high teenage pregnancy rate, high rate of unwed births, high intra-family violence, high unemployment, etc.

What is important about this transformation since 1960

is that a realistic understanding of the black "family culture milieu" must factor in these crucial social class dynamics. Nowadays black parents—father or mother—raise their children according to their particular class structure—that is, according to their opportunities and resources. To portray black parenting without factoring in the element of class structure is inadequate. Black parenting in the 1990s has been changed irrevocably by the major social class recomposition within black American life.

Interface of Black Parenting and Black Biography

My particular experience at black parenting cannot be understood without some personal background. I entered the black bourgeoisie (the "mobile strata") as a professional scholar upon receiving my Ph.D. in political science at Harvard University in 1959. I came from a clan of Free Negro families—on both my maternal and paternal sides—that reaches back to the 1820s in Eastern Shore Maryland. My mother's grandfather was a Free Negro who settled in Philadelphia before the Civil War and enlisted in the U.S. 24th Colored Infantry Regiment, joining the War for Negro Freedom. He was a carpenter and, along with other former Civil War colored soldiers, settled outside Philadelphia in the 1870s and organized small black communities, one of which (Ambler, Pennsylvania) became my hometown. My father's great-grandfather—Reverend Issac Lee—had founded the first African Methodist Episcopal church in Kent County, Maryland, in the 1840s, and my father became an ordained clergyman in another branch of African Methodism in the early 1920s—the African Methodist United Protestant Church, founded among black artisans in 1816. My father spent part of his career ministering to an African Methodist United Protestant church in my hometown that was founded in 1885 by my mother's grandfather—Jacob Laws.

My parents had seven children—four daughters and three sons—and I was the fourth oldest child. By virtue of my father's clergyman occupation (the black community had two other clergymen) and my mother's family pedigree—the granddaughter of a black Civil War veteran, a carpenter, and home builder, and founder of the oldest black church in the community, which included inheriting several houses owned by her grandfather (from which rent during the Depression of the 1930s was important to our family income)—I was reared in the black middle-class. My mother had an authoritative standing in the black community, one that was deeper than my father's, and as I reflect back on my family, I remember tension between my parents on this matter. I say *tension* advisedly, because I don't recall ever any open conflict. But the tension was real, and my parents divorced when I was an adolescent, during World War II. The Conference of the African Methodist United Protestant Church, headquartered since the 1830s in Wilmington, Delaware, relocated my father to another African Methodist United Protestant church in Delaware.

This background affected my own parenting in a number of respects. For one, I had an understanding of black middle-class parenting patterns. Unlike some middle-class black friends of mine who entered the black bourgeoisie from lower-class or working-class backgrounds and were naive or romantic about the dynamics of middle-class black families, believing especially that bourgeois black families are "tension-free" or "conflict-free," I had no such illusions. Of course, an intrinsic grasp of the bourgeois black family is no guarantee against crises in one's own parenting journey. Two of my sisters got divorced, and one sister divorced twice. Yet, things being equal, middle-class blacks entering parenting from middle-class backgrounds have a bag of precedents, a bag of experiences, to draw upon when tensions and conflicts arise, if, of course they are intelligent and disciplined enough to draw upon them.

Thus, in key areas of potential tension (like managing family income, hints or evidence of infidelity, handling of adolescent crises—especially those of female children—etc.), a bag of precedents from a middle class Black family background can be enormously helpful. One condition of such utility is, I think, candor about oneself and one's surroundings—attributes I discovered were scarce among the middle-class black males I attended undergraduate college with in the early 1950s—at an all-male black college, Lincoln University (Pennsylvania). They shared the delusion of their parents (fathers mainly) that middle-class black males had a distinctly lower rate of male infidelity compared to lower-class blacks. Although in the social science literature on African-American life during the first fifty years of this century this outlook was often recorded (see, for example, Hortense Powdermaker, *After Freedom* [1939]), a more realistic perspective on the stability of middle-class black households in that era is that middle-class black spouses endured marital infidelity to ensure the broader social security of a stable middle-class household.

I recently examined some data on the family patterns among my peers of the early 1950s period, and found that some fifty percent were divorced or separated. Of course, the usual sources of conflict between marital partners could have triggered my college cohorts' high rate of family instability rather than infidelity. Certainly they were part of that enormous expansion of black professionals from the mid-1960s onward. They were, in fact, the first group of black college graduates to join the mainstream of bourgeois white Americans. And our spouses were the first college-educated women to have career opportunities that had been previously reserved exclusively for men. Such fundamental social and gender transformations inevitably became potential sources of marital tension or conflict.

The Multicultural Milieu and Black Parenting

My generation was also the first to enjoy all the options of the wider society. Just as the 1950s and 1960s brought middle-class options to second-generation white ethnic groups (Irish, Jewish, and Italian especially), such as choice of college (Princeton rather than Notre Dame or Boston College, for example), inter-ethnic dating and marriage choices, and access to WASP law firms and businesses, college-educated African-Americans from the late 1960s onward also had more opportunities. To attend white colleges and professional schools, blacks of my age cohort did have to depend upon public-policy assistance.

Also, to enter major professional job markets, they did need the support of affirmative action programs. Nonetheless, a wide range of possibilities have been available to thousands on thousands of middle-class African-Americans for a good thirty years now, and black parenting experiences have been affected by this sea change.

In my own case, and that of other persons of my age, one of the multicultural options was choosing a white bourgeois spouse. In the summer of 1959, when I received my Ph.D., I also received a sizable research fellowship from the Ford Foundation to conduct research for a year and a half in West Africa. Before departing on that research project, I married a white graduate student in anthropology—Marion Dusser De Barenne—and together we headed for West Africa. Our first child, Jennifer, was born in 1963, and over the next three years we had two more (Peter and Hannah). Black professionals of my age group, say from fifty-five to sixty-five years old, saw a significant increase in interracial and inter-ethnic marriage. Why? For many reasons, of course, but in part because we, along with our white liberal and progressive conferees, were the Civil Rights movement generation. My list of black friends and colleagues who chose interracial marriage includes Wilbur Tatum, Marian Edelman, Roger Wilkins, Jamaica Kincaid, and Ishmael Reed, among many others.

Thus, I raised my children to be fully conscious of both their black and white heritage. One might say, what else could you have done, Kilson? Well, believe it or not, there are biracial or inter-ethnic couples who expose their children to only one culture, be it racial or ethnic. Marion, for example, has a niece who married a Jewish American whose parents fashioned monocultural parenting boundaries for their children—a pattern that happens currently to less than ten percent of gentile-Jewish marriages (overall, just over fifty percent of Jewish marriages are now gentile-Jewish). I also had a close black professional friend who was a military intelligence officer and married to a European literary scholar. Since his white wife was a retiring sort, my black ethnocentric friend fashioned a rather twisted monocultural parenting framework for his three children.

I would not say that my parenting style followed a formal design. Rather, it was forthright but open-ended, even hit-and-miss. My children learned from me when they were quite young that they, in one of their biological and cultural dimensions, were black, and thus shared a heritage of white supremacist oppression, victimization, defamation, and marginalization. Early on I and Marion informed them of the meaning of their phenotype attributes—their skin color, their mixture of straight and curly hair, etc., and took them often to their relatives on my side: to their grandfather's church and farm in Kent County, Maryland; to their great-great grandfather Jacob Laws' church and also their grandmother's church in Ambler, Pennsylvania; to their business manager uncle William Lawrence Kilson in Philadelphia; to their cabinet-maker uncle Richard Dennis Kilson in Philadelphia; to their gospel singer aunt Bernice Kilson Davis in Wilmington, Delaware, and so forth. To this day my children recall vividly the gospels sung with vigor and pain by their aunt Bernice at their grandmother Louisa Laws Kilson's funeral, held in a lovely old stone African Methodist United Protestant church that their great-great grandfather founded in 1885 and helped to build with his own hands. I made certain my children's African-American heritage was available to them.

And I use *available* advisedly. For it was neither in my own middle-class black rearing nor a part of my adult African-American persona to evangelize the black component of their identity. Put another way, a sense of tradition shaped and aided me toward a *black perspective that was forthright about race realities, on the one hand, but operationally pragmatic on the other hand.* That sense of tradition extended back in time to a long-standing black socialization experience of Free Negro households in Eastern Shore communities of early nineteenth-century Maryland—the same Free Negro communities that forged Frederick Douglass.

Thus, given this orientation, I emphasized, above all, norms of fairness and work ethic, achievement, and accountability (that is, outreach to black needs). Then I let my children synthesize these elements as they would. As I reflect back on this, I recall more similarities than differences in the way my children responded. In middle school and secondary school in Lexington, Massachusetts, during the 1970s, when hyper-black consciousness patterns were broadcast among African-Americans, each of my children were swept up to some degree. Most visibly, each had a variant of the "Afro" hairstyle. Each had a racially mixed group of friends. Each was good at athletics— ice skating, lacrosse, basketball, swimming, baseball—and since Lexington was well represented in the Metco School Busing Program (it brought working-class black children to Lexington's schools—schools that were overwhelmingly middle-class and upper-middle-class), there were a fair number of black students in the Lexington high school to befriend. During basketball season (both girls' and boys') the Kilson house was a beehive of activity among my children and their black teammates, with sometimes as many as ten of them sleeping over Friday or Saturday night because of practices or games.

The white side of their heritage was also available to my children. Marion's family lived either in Massachusetts or in nearby New Hampshire. When they were between two and six, my children lived in Marion's sister's house on Garden Street in Cambridge—Aunt Thea's house. Marion's aunt was often a surrogate parent to my children, parenting them for several months at a time while Marion and I were off researching in West Africa. My children frequently attended weekend dinners and lunches, among other family gatherings of the Dusser de Barrenes, Greenes, and Lockwoods—branches of Marion's clan. And, of course, they had white friends. The first child to be married, Jennifer, married an African-American who was born in Britain of Caribbean parents but raised in the United States. The second child to marry, Hannah, married a Scotsman. My son, Peter, who studied business management at the University of Massachusetts and economics in France, is unmarried, presently heading up the swimming program at the Roxbury YMCA and assists in YMCA fund-raising.

Concluding Note: Importance of Accountability

Let me conclude with a brief note on the importance of the third element of my parenting of biracial children: accountability. This is crucial because of the powerful tendency of those moving up from "outsider" or pariah status to converge with mainstream attitudes and preferences. As noted earlier, the significant middle-class growth among blacks since the late 1960s has not extended to some thirty-five percent of black families who are weak working-class and poor. So successful blacks have, I insist, a certain accountability toward poor African-Americans. And this outreach applies as well to that vicious affront to black folks' honor associated with a persistent kind of white supremacist culture lag in American society—namely, a societal resistance to cross-racial fraternization, a resistance especially strong still among white Americans but mirrored too in the behavior of some Latino Americans and especially Asian Americans. A major measure of this culture lag is the still low rate of cross-racial marriages involving a black American partner in a period when nearly all major non-black ethnic groups intermarry at least thirty-five percent of the time. The rate among white ethnic groups like Italians, Irish Americans, and Jewish Americans is around fifty percent. White supremacist perceptions toward black Americans still remain active as well in making friends, and so the goal of accountability involves challenging these perceptions.

In this connection, I was attentive back in May 1995 when a group of biracial or multicultural black students at Harvard College announced the formation of a new student organization that would attempt to reduce the inner tension some biracial students experience between the claims from the black heritage, on one side, and the white heritage, on the other. I sensed something both naive and disingenuous in this group's formulation of their announcement of a new organization. So I sat down and penned a reaction to this announcement in the form of a letter to the *Harvard Crimson*.

In my letter I first remarked that this tension of "double consciousness" that biracial students now say they experience is of long vintage, for earlier generations of those then called mulattos experienced the same, and under more vicious forms of white supremacist patterns in American life than obtain today. Henry Louis Gates, Jr., recently observed in an article on Frederick Douglass in the *New York Times Book Review* how this great figure of black-white parentage exhibited this "double consciousness." In early attempts at an autobiography, Douglass emphasized the fact that his father was a white slave owner, but in a later attempt Douglass highlighted the importance of his black mother. From W. E. B. Du Bois (founder of the NAACP), to James Weldon Johnson (head of NAACP in the 1920s), to Jean Toomer (a major novelist of the New Negro Movement in the twenties and thirties), to many, many more leading black figures, there has been a perpetual juggling of meanings of self stemming from one's biracial or multicultural realities.

Today's students of mixed black heritage are not experiencing anything new. Today's biracial students do, however, have an obligation rooted in the many contributions and sacrifices by earlier generations. Fulfilling this obligation is, in my perspective, quite open-ended in regard to method, means, timing, etc. There is no set of rules or items of an action agenda. Rather, it is an orientation toward life, and as such you fulfill it in your everyday professional work in business, law, banking, the academy, etc., tilting when you can toward fairness and toward egalitarian ends.

Today's college-educated blacks can do more than penetrate the American mainstream. The whole thrust of the pragmatic-activist perspective among mainstream black intelligentsia has always been to maximize this American power-center penetration in tandem with racial democratizing goals equally important to black life. The white supremacist tradition still makes pariahs of far too many African-Americans (and of Hispanics and Asian Americans, too). It is not honorable for the new generation of black students and professionals to do anything less.

Michael G. Hanchard

On "Good" Black Fathers

Michaeal Hanchard is a professor of political science at Northwestern University. He is the author of Orpheus and Power: Afro-Brazilian Social Movements in Rio de Janeiro and Sao Paolo, Brazil, 1945–1988, *and has written on a variety of topics in the areas of social theory and cultural criticism. He is currently working on a project on race, modernity, and the politics of the African diaspora.*

After observing my then two-year-old daughter and me playing with each other at a summer event during graduate school, a black woman graduate student I knew walked up to us with a big smile and said, "It's so nice to see a black man who spends so much time with his child," adding in a serious tone that reduced her voice to a conspiratorial whisper: "There's not too many black men who spend time with their children these days, you know," before she walked away. My daughter, oblivious to the exchange, continued with her demand that I flip her one more time (for the third time!). I was stunned.

How could this woman make such a statement, I thought to myself, when she herself was a product of a household with a responsible father (of whom she often spoke)? Had the dynamics of black communities—middle- and working-class—changed that much over the course of one generation to make the term *black father* an oxymoron, and cavorting with my daughter an exception? Like many other people in the United States, black or otherwise, I had heard and read the statistics and data on the number of black men who helped produce children but who were not "heading households," which has come to be understood as not living with the mother of his child. This has also come to be equated with, I believe, being an absent, irresponsible, or non-parent.

These two assumptions are not, however, only part of the rhetoric about the crisis of black fatherhood. They are inextricably related to more general assumptions about fatherhood, domesticity, and masculinity in these United States. Rarely, though, are discussions about black fatherhood linked to a broader conjuncture of societal forces that have shaped the present moment. Consequently, relations between black women, black men, and their children are rarely considered against the backdrop of rising divorce rates, family dysfunction, and cultural conservatism in the nation as a whole.

Embedded in my fellow graduate students' comments to me during that afternoon barbecue were parts of this discussion, the presumptions about the culpability of black men in impeding our ability to reproduce and nurture ourselves. That moment in which I was identified as a presence in my daughter's life became a barometer and lightning rod for black male parenting. In contrast to most mothers I know, who are automatically considered parents, young fathers like myself who are also parents are often treated like some sort of novelty. The fact of my blackness made my public act of parenting seem like an even greater novelty. While the widely voiced concern can be attributed to the circumstances under which black men, as fathers and individuals, find themselves at the present time, it is also a variation on a recurrent theme over the course of U.S. history, politics, and public policy about the very ability of African-Americans to care for themselves as a people, from slave quarters in Mississippi to the south side of Chicago, from Strivers Row in Harlem to Shaker Heights in Cleveland and points elsewhere. Whereas once African-Americans, like other people of African descent, were considered intellectually incapable of attending to their own self-governance, they are now interpreted by many who hold conservative as well as liberal positions as being culturally incapable—that is, without the moral and ethical imperatives—to raise and take care of families. The so-called "crisis of the black male," a topic of debate among members of black communities and their attendant institutions, policy makers, the religious right, rap musicians, and others, is often segregated from society at large by a language that assumes that black men and the communities that spawned them can be interpreted only through the lens of slavery and discrimination, as if these two features of U.S. society and culture affected only black people.

As those of any color who are involved in the lives of children know, parenting involves much more than an afternoon barbecue or any other public event in which people who supposedly love one another perform the usual niceties of hugging, kissing, and embracing in ways that suggest to the world outside that all is well within. Biographies of celebrities both living and dead, talk shows, television documentaries, and published research by specialists on families have provided ample grounds for suggesting that while the image of a loving, mutually supportive family with two ever present parents is not an absolute myth, there are few actual families that resemble the conventional, "traditional" model of the nuclear family. At the same time, those individuals and families whose lives do not resemble the mythic family are not, by definition, either bad people or bad parents.

Most people fall somewhere in between the models for families that more closely resemble a facade on a Hollywood movie lot than an actual case of domesticity or the entirely dysfunctional ensembles of disfigured humanity that family arrangements sometimes turn out to be. Most parents struggle with issues of divorce, fidelity, time and budgetary constraints, ornery relatives, and other thorny subjects within the context of their families and individual identities. Black people are no different.

What does distinguish black fathers, mothers, and their children from the present "crisis of the family" is that black people have struggled through various crisis and moments—as families and individuals—ever since their arrival into the New World as slaves four centuries ago. The very condition of slavery presupposed the absence or negation of family, since slavery operated on the premise that slaves belonged to no one other than slave owners themselves. From the dawn of slavery, people of African descent in the United States resisted their comprehensive but incomplete domination at the hands of slave masters by maintaining whatever possible links with family members on other plantations, or by forging familial ties where there were none, such as those between shipmates and their offspring.

I briefly recall this history simply to suggest that the present "crisis" of the black family in general and black males in particular has a prior history, and it is but a variation on a theme. With this in mind, I would like to make a basic point about the need to recognize the creative responses African-American communities have had to the responsibilities of fatherhood that have not fit within the parameters of the mythic constructions of fatherhood, the family, masculinity, and domesticity. Discussions of black fatherhood that attempt to force black males into a model of parenting that few people—male or female—white, black, or otherwise, adhere to in the contemporary United States should be viewed with suspicion against this historical and contemporary backdrop. Unfortunately, as my own personal example suggests, members of the African-American community, often in an effort to portray a sense of the cohesiveness and respectability so often denied by broader society, reproduce the same myths about parenting and family responsibility that imprison them within the very stereotypes they have been struggling for so long to break free of.

While I do not want to suggest that we ignore or dismiss nasty legacies of domestic and other forms of violence within black communities, teenage pregnancies, and a litany of other maladies that have been perpetrated and perpetuated by black men, I do want to suggest that we view discussions about the "crisis of the black male" with skepticism as long as the more general crises weighing over black people are ignored. Ultimately, the debates about the black male are less about black maleness and responsibility than about the variety of racially and economically discriminatory circumstances, both inside and outside black communities, that black males often find themselves in and react to, regardless of their parenting status.

An example of the ways in which the stereotypes of black dysfunction plague even the most successful black families regardless of their specific circumstances again comes from a personal experience, involving a girlfriend of my daughter. This child, whom I will call Rachel, was my daughter's best friend in the first grade. Donna (for the purposes of this essay), Rachel's mother, was a hardworking woman. She not only raised Rachel but worked at a demanding managerial job, held leadership positions in church and community organizations, and raised her stepson's infant daughter in her home. Neither Donna nor her husband were wealthy by any means, but they were able to provide not only for themselves but for their extended family as well, in both material and spiritual terms. They lived in a modest one-family home in the black section of a very segregated city. Donna would sometimes allow several days to pass before reading through the material in the school folder that Rachel brought home every day, which included past homework and exercises as well as information about upcoming school events. Like most working parents I know, regardless of socioeconomic status, it was a constant struggle to juggle domestic and professional responsibilities. With perhaps the exception of male single parents, I believe it is safe to say that women parents have greater home responsibilities than their male counterparts, and Donna was no exception.

Ms. Mason, her daughter's teacher, reprimanded Rachel one day for not having her folder materials checked by a parent, one of the rules of her classroom. After receiving a note from Rachel's teacher on the matter, Donna immediately called my wife and told her something like the following: "The next time I brought Rachel to school, I had a talk with the teacher, to let her know that just because I hadn't looked at her folder did not mean I didn't check her homework," adding "because I'm a good black parent."

A good black parent. What does this mean? There are several connotations that these four words could imply. A black person cannot simply be a parent; they are a black parent. But to be a black parent is simply not enough; one must be a good black parent. How does being a good black parent differ from being a good white parent, or simply a white or any other hued parent? What links Donna and me in this example is the manner in which both of us lurk between the categories already created for us and acted upon in a racist society. The identities of our lives are multiple: parent, spouse, counsel, friend, son and daughter, and so on. The stereotypes that we supposedly inhabit are singular: suspect parent. We are suspect parents because we are suspect human beings, suspected by the ideologies of racial discrimination to be something less than the norm, less than ideal.

Donna is a prime example of how black people both in and out of conventional families respond to these stereotypes of negativity. There is little doubt, I think, in her statement about her ability to be a good parent or the ability of others in her position to do the same. There is doubt, though, about the capability of certain members of white society to see her that way. This, unfortunately, is part of the legacy of black performance in public life in the United States. One of the cultural responses of blacks in virtually every profession since emancipation has been that black people must be nearly perfect in their undertakings, lest a little slip-up here or there (unchecked class assignments, for example) be taken as not only individual incompetence but a collective shortcoming. This is echoed in the personal narratives and biographies of people like Benjamin O. Davis of the U.S. Army, sports legends Jackie Robinson and Joe Louis, performers like Wilma Rudolph and Lena Horne. It is also echoed in everyday people's daily lives, as Donna's example illustrates.

The example of her life is instructive because of the way in which it combines the activities of both conventional nuclear and extended families (community, in a word) that extends beyond narrower definitions of family. First, given the realities of teenage pregnancy, the ravages of crack, undereducation, unemployment, and other plagues of working-class black communities, black mothers and fathers cannot afford—I repeat, cannot afford—to operate exclusively under the nuclear family rubric. In no way am I declaring myself "anti-family" in the way that political and cultural conservatives claim that leftists advocate. I realize that families of all colors have had to adjust and adapt to the changing realities of the 1990s in the United States, where even middle- and upper-middle-class parents no longer operate with the assurance that their children will be able to fare as well as or better than they have. Black communities must not allow the focus on "the crisis of the black family" to obscure the larger problems of this precarious time. Simply put, if the majority of U.S. communities, which includes African-Americans, are neither products of nor participants in a two-parent family, then why should African-Americans be expected to adhere to a more restrictive notion of family that serves as an ideal more than a reality and, ultimately, was designed with another group of people in mind?

All this relates to the politics of black fatherhood since, invariably, black men who sire and/or nurture children can be fathers only in relation to their children, husbands and/or lovers in relation to their wives and/or companions, sons in relation to their parents. When viewed in isolation, black fatherhood becomes a fetish of machismo and conventional masculinity rather than a practical component of family life within immediate and extended families and communities. When viewed in isolation, the black family becomes but another receptacle for dominant values and ideals that do not work for the dominant social group in the first place but are utilized to tell African-Americans, once again, that they don't measure up.

A recent example of the effects of distorted images upon African-American males comes from the state of New Jersey, where Republican governor Christine Whitman started a controversy in March 1995 during an interview when she stated that young black ghetto men in Newark proudly considered siring children out of wedlock a matter of adding "jewels to the crown." Ms. Whitman, who is certainly no ghetto dweller, obtained this information from a black mother in Newark who informed her that this was the reality of black male parental responsibility in that city.

The governor has had to respond to the outcry over this statement from a variety of sources in black communities in New Jersey, including young black fathers who have children out of wedlock and are responsible parents. Participants in the Young Fathers' Program in

Newark,* a program that had been in existence eight years prior to Ms. Whitman's statement, as well as other collectives of young fathers, have informed the governor of the seriousness of their programs and their good-parenting practices regardless of their marital status. In a meeting with the governor in June of the same year, several members of the Young Fathers' Program and lifelong Newark residents told Ms. Whitman that they had never heard of the "jewels in the crown" phrase uttered by the young black mother.

At various times in the ensuing months, the governor reiterated that she had been merely repeating something said to her. It was a statement she neither confirmed or endorsed. During her June meeting with Young Fathers' Program participants, she stated, "I didn't stigmatize anybody."

While she may have made what one would call an "honest mistake" (certainly impolitic), she still misses the point, but she does so in a way that is useful for this article. Those young men were already stigmatized by the fact that they did not operate within the conventional two-family model. Her statement, to my mind, can be viewed only as naive or disingenuous when seen in the context of two arenas of public debate that relate to this

---

* The Young Fathers' Program was founded in 1987 after a successful pilot program initiated in 1986. The program, which is housed in the New Jersey Medical School in Newark, is designed to assist young black and latino men between fifteen and twenty-three in meeting the emotional, financial, and social demands of fatherhood. Its services include educational and employment training for young men and their families, family support, and counseling to reduce the risk of neglect and abuse within these families. As of June 1995, approximately one thousand young fathers have utilized the program's services. For more information contact (201) 982-5277.

controversy, family values and the disintegration of the black family.

More subtle indignations, however, emerge when we consider the fact that a white, female governor who presides over some of the most blighted and underfunded cities in the entire country would accept the comments of one person of any race to characterize the behavior of an entire class of individuals. Would she have relayed these comments in such an offhand, unmediated manner if the individuals in question were young white men from Princeton or Upper Montclair, New Jersey, two of the state's most affluent neighborhoods? Would she have even believed the comments of a single person from the neighborhood? We may never know the answer to these two questions, but it is significant that in most cases involving white parenting such questions are rarely posed. My guess is that part of the reason she relied so easily upon one black mother's depiction of unwed fathers is because it corresponded so easily with common assumptions about young black men.

Tellingly, in her June 1995 meeting with the program participants she explained that her statement was a rendering of "a comment that someone said to me, by someone who said this was what happened, whether it was on her block or what, I don't know." Ironically, her explanation reveals the pressures of what I shall call "racial translation," which are often imposed upon blacks in their interaction with whites in the United States. Before making such a statement, wouldn't it have made sense for Ms. Whitman to determine whether her informant was talking about young black men in general or a few on the woman's block? This is a depressingly familiar scenario in which the comments of one black individual as "racial translator" become the opinion or depiction of black people as a whole, much in the same way that the negative actions of one or several black individuals are often perceived as being symptomatic of black communities or the entire black race.

The similarities between the responses of these young black fathers and Donna are striking. Both felt the need to respond to others' characterizations that did not correspond with the realities of their daily lives. Like my own identity as a father, their identities as parents reside somewhere in between stereotypes and the starkest cases of parental neglect and abuse. What distinguishes these young men from Donna and myself is that poverty, undereducation, and unemployment render them socially naked. They do not have the trappings of middle-class respectability that would shield them from the accusations and characterizations of irresponsibility in the way that middle-class whites or minorities do. One only has to think of the surprise and shock echoed in voices and journalistic reports when a case of middle-class abuse is uncovered (parents who lock their infant children in the house to go on a vacation, for example) to obtain a sense of what notions of middle-class respectability can obscure. This is not restricted to young black men, either; the poor in general are symbolically victimized by these characterizations, as they are deemed to be the underside of what good parenting is all about.

In an age where both parents work and only three percent of families in the United States rely solely on a male breadwinner, parents who live with their children don't always have ample time to spend with them. In many middle- and upper-middle-class households (black and white) it is not uncommon to find nannies performing the functions of parents, who spend less and less time at home. Years of neglect and inattention have taken their toll on many prep school-educated Ivy League-bound adolescents, just as it has upon the "latchkey" children in working-class homes who are alone, locked inside their homes while their parents are at work. I mention these things to suggest what should be an obvious point; *no class or race has a monopoly on good or bad parenting.* Seemingly "external" societal factors have as much impact upon family dynamics as internal ones.

When one adds relational discord, physical and psycho-emotional violence, incest, alcoholism, poverty, depression, and a range of other personal travails that have domestic repercussions, some children are better off without their biological or adoptive parents. This further erodes the all-or-nothing distinctions made between parents who live with their children and those who do not. The behavioral imprint left upon children in dysfunctional households can affect not only immediate family members but successive generations as well. With males of any color, children who witnessed or experienced physical and non-physical violence are likely to reproduce such violence in their own families.

At a conference in Fort Lauderdale, Florida, in October 1994, six present and former professional football players—all black—participated in a forum on domestic violence against women. Having witnessed their fathers break the arms and blacken the eyes of their mothers and traumatize everyone in their presence at the same time, several of these men in turn heaped similar forms of violence upon their girlfriends and spouses. This cycle, as these men came to recognize, has to be broken before there are any realistic prospects for improved family dynamics among people of African descent. The reason I mention these particular men is to suggest that such labels, for example, "wife beater," could apply to a broad array of males, from the aforementioned men to O. J. Simpson. Eradicating domestic and other forms of intra-community violence often means coming to terms with memories of violence inflicted upon them by a previous generation—by mothers, fathers, relatives, or family friends.

To discuss "the black family" without consideration of the myriad forms of violence and its consequences for black men as well as black women is to engage in the sort of blissful denial of negative, abusive "family values" that have existed as long as families have. Such violence has often operated as a primary cause of drug abuse, predation by young males, teenage runaways, suicide, depression, among other phenomena that characterize what family specialists refer to as "at-risk youth." If we are concerned with the preservation of family values—"African," "Afro-Centric," or otherwise—let us make sure about just what it is we are preserving.

Here is where more complex understandings of the relationship between family and community become crucial for deeper probings of the politics of black fatherhood. In much of black conservative discussions about responsibility for teenage pregnancy (public statements and writings by Stanley Crouch and Glenn Loury provide two examples), there is often a nostalgic evocation of a bygone era when young women were sanctioned within black communities for having children out of wedlock. Suspending for the moment whether this was actually true even in some (certainly not all) black communities, or whether this was or is viable coping strategy for young teenage mothers, there is virtually no mention in this rhetoric of popular community sanctions against woman beaters or men who too readily and too violently spank their children. Should this nostalgic rhetoric be preserved? Should the silence about these issues be preserved? As usual, women political and cultural activists remain at the forefront of this discussion within the black community. Byllye Avery, founder of the National Black Women's Health Project, is one example of a black woman political activist who has worked on these issues, often to the deaf ears of her male counterparts in the struggle for racial equality. Queen Latifah and Karyn White, two popular contemporary artists, have both produced effective music and videos on the theme of domestic violence within black families.* Certainly there are other forums, created largely by black women, that address domestic-violence issues, but there needs to be an ongoing dialogue about these issues in black communities and institutions. Family coherence should not be confused with individual abuse, intimidation, and oppression. Nor should discussion of the failings of particular black men in this regard be automatically considered a threat to the black male.

All of these concerns, from notions of community and

* See Queen Latifah's 1993 hit "U.N.I.T.Y." and Karyn White's incisive 1994 production, aptly entitled "I'd Rather Be Alone." Both ably capture the problems inherent in static categorizations of the nuclear family which do not address the reasons why, in some instances, it is healthier for people not to be in their nuclear family relationships, ones that cause unnecessary emotional and physical disfigurement.

extended families to domestic violence, impact upon black fathers and the politics of their being. An example of this occurred while I was riding a bus one day with two young black men from a summer program, which I was mentoring. I became the mediator in an argument about "proper" parenting philosophies for black men, a discussion that was prompted, I believe, by the presence of my daughter Jenna.

One young man from Kentucky stated that if he were a parent, he would raise his boy and girl children differently since boys, men in the making, had to be taught not to cry, not wear their emotions on their sleeves and commit other acts that would make them be perceived as weak. In contrast, the other young man, who hailed from Boston, said that he would not raise his girl child any differently from his son, since men too need to cry and express their emotions. "Plus" he added with emphasis, "it's rough out here on the sisters these days. They've got to be tough too. They need all the help they can get."

And so they do. The task for progressive black males, as fathers, lovers, friends, and "brothers" in both senses of the term, is to understand black masculinity as merely one facet of their humanity. Like me, these two young men exist somewhere in between negative stereotypes and ideal-types. Together, in dialogue, they were not only coming to terms with what it meant to be responsible black men in the contemporary United States, but with what it meant to be fuller human beings.

Henry Louis Gates, Jr.

Considerations on Fatherhood

Henry Louis Gates, Jr., is the W. E. B. Du Bois Professor of the Humanities and Chair of the Afro-American Studies Department at Harvard University, and Director of the W. E. B. Du Bois Institute for Afro-American Research at Harvard. Among his books are the bestselling Colored People: A Memoir, The Signifying Monkey: A Theory of Afro-American Literary Criticism, *and* Loose Cannons: Notes on the Culture Wars. *He is a frequent contributor to* The New Yorker *magazine.*

When I found out that my wife was pregnant for the first time, my feelings were quite complicated. I was overcome by a profound sense of joy and excitement, but also I felt a tremendous anxiety after the initial exhilaration wore off. In retrospect, I realized that this was because I wanted to be a good provider. I did not want my children to have to struggle for the basic necessities of life. Here I was, merely an assistant professor, twenty-nine years old, had barely finished my dissertation, without tenure, I suddenly thought, "Oh, my God, now I have this child who I want to go to Harvard, and I want to be able to pay for it!"

Still, the happiest day of my life, bar none, was the day my first child was born. My wife, Sharon, went through eighteen hours of labor; then they had to induce labor, and then take the baby with a C-section. Finally—miraculously—there was this beautiful baby, and I was just floating on air. It was the happiest day of my life.

I had started preparing for this miracle before it arrived. The first thing I did was to go to Lamaze class. Second, I channeled all my anxiety into work and career. To counter all the fears I had about being a good provider, I started working harder and trying to make more money. I figured I'd be a nice father and that I could manage to love in an emotionally balanced way, so I wasn't worried about that. I was even certain that my housework skills would suffice, so I did not worry about those either. But I had anxiety about being able to provide materially.

However anxious I felt back then, it never occurred to me, however, that I would be a *bad* provider. I came from a very stable family. I had dinner with my mother and father every day for practically eighteen years. I also had a very close extended family that lived all around me— nine uncles and three aunts, most of whom lived down the street—so my world centered around family. Ultimately I knew we would make it because my support systems were strong. I had been trained, by many rich examples in my own family, about how to be kind and loving, and I never worried about whether I would be sensitive to my children, especially if they were intelligent, high-spirited kids.

As it turned out, I had an intelligent, high-spirited girl. When I was a teenager and a young man, I only wanted boys—I could only imagine having boys. Yet when we had a girl, all of a sudden I couldn't remember that I ever wanted to have a boy. I love having girls. (I now have two.) I get to tell them about boys, what dogs they are, and not to trust them, and not to confuse passion with love. I think I'm good with my girls. One time I heard Gloria Naylor say that she wanted more black women to have fathers who were professionals because it taught them a lot about dealing with the world. That has stuck with me for a long time.

Being a father allows you to reconnect with your own history in an intricate sort of way. I remember as a teenager I had strong sexual desires that I couldn't do anything with, so I figure as adolescent girls that they're just like me, and I'm kind of cool about that. Certainly, I don't want them to get hurt and I don't want them sleeping with the football team or anything, but I know that they have to go out and go to parties. So we have rules and I want them to stick to the rules. But I want them to be strong, independent, and to work hard, and not allow themselves to be victims of sexism—my own or society's. That is very important to me. Women are clearly stereotyped. You can even see it in the eighth grade—boys go on one track and girls tend to go on another. That kind of stuff worries me, and I don't understand how any man who has daughters cannot be a feminist. As a father you have to stomp on anybody who doesn't treat them as equals, and talk to them truthfully, about everything.

I can't imagine a more intimate relationship than the one I have with my daughters. I talk to them as equals. I love them. I mean, they're really smart, and I want them to thrive in this society. And the only way to do that is to show them an example—for me to thrive in this society—and encourage them to be articulate and speak out, and to demand their rights and not be demure. Resisting stereotypes is something that we as black people understand, but often we as black males don't understand about black women. I try to teach them not to use race as a shield or an excuse, but when somebody crosses the racist or sexist line, tell them about it.

There are added complications because Sharon is white, but having interracial kids really does not consciously

affect my parenting—I never think about it. I think about
their mother as a person with a set of characteristics; I
never think her as a *white* woman. I think of her as
Sharon. I don't act any differently with my girls than I
would if they were not biracial. They're black as far as
the law's concerned. It doesn't matter. I could have married a light-complected black woman, and they could
have been even lighter!

That isn't to say that race is completely meaningless,
in their lives or in mine. It's just that it can't be the prominent force in our relationship. I can recall a troubling
experience I had with one father. Once I was riding
in the backseat of a car, listening to a very prominent
African-American man scolding his son. His boy was either singing some song, or using a phrase, that the father
said was not black. I remember thinking, "That's a horrible thing to do." I mean, as far as I'm concerned, there
are thirty-five million ways to be black. However the
black child turns out, that's what blackness is. It was clear
that the man had anxiety about the boy not being accepted by his peers and that he clearly had an abstract
idea of what blackness was. Blackness doesn't exist when
you're dealing with a father and a daughter or a father
and a son, or maybe it does, but it's somewhere offstage.
The main thing is the father-child relationship; everything
else, including race, is secondary.

I don't really have to push race into my daughters'
faces; it manifests itself whenever it comes up in my own
life. And when things happen to them, they bring it to
the dinner table and then we talk about it. I didn't want
to be one of those parents that says, "Crispus Attucks was
the first black man to . . ."—giving them a history lesson

every day. They would have hated it. Kids want you to
sit down and watch cartoons with them. And I figure they
get that history in school.

So race hasn't been the major issue between my girls
and me. What *has* been an issue is that I work so hard.
One time someone asked me something like, "What percentage of your time is work, and what percentage is just
personal?" I said, I don't have a personal life. I don't. All
I think about is my writing, my teaching, and my work.
I'm very much preoccupied with my work—I really love
it and I often have to force myself to remember that I have
a family. This was not an easy adjustment at the very beginning of my career precisely because I felt driven to
work ten times harder.

My nightmare as a father is to see my daughter graduate from Wellesley, give the commencement address,
and thank her mother and not thank her father. My
daughters are my heart, and I really want them to love
me. Yet because I'm gone so much of the time, I wonder
if I have the type of impact that I'd like to have. Toni
Morrison once said that she would not have wanted herself as a mother because she's a writer, and writers are, by
definition, too selfish. I think academics are also too selfish. Vocational sacrifices lead to a lot of compromises, and
I'm sure that my being away so much has had some kind
of effect on me and them. My wife is home every day
just as my mother and father were. I would have hated
having a father like me. I might have been proud of him,
but it's like saluting the flag or something—empty. The
bottom line is, where were you when I came home and I
needed help with that geometry? My answer is: I was in
Ohio giving a lecture. There's a trade-off, but I wouldn't

do it any differently. I like the life I have, and I hope that as my children get older they'll understand. But those are the breaks. I don't want to be a "picket fence," *Leave It to Beaver* daddy, that's not me. I wasn't raised to do that. Yet it is a profoundly difficult choice to make. It is a sacrifice. My only salvation is my hope that my children will grow up successfully, understand me, and become like me. Then their children and I, like the joke says, will have a common enemy. I think if I live long enough they'll have more sympathy for me and what I am trying to do in the world, just as I came to have more sympathy for my parents when I had kids. When they have careers and they realize that food and clothes don't magically appear, I hope they will begin to appreciate my choices.

Given this drive to excel, I have had to learn how to not be domineering with my children. One important aspect of becoming a father is the recognition that you have to find emotionally positive ways to express your strength. You realize this when you hold your newborn in your arms. It becomes clear to you, in a visceral way, that you can't hold them too tightly because they are so delicate. But learning that psychologically is a lot more difficult, and it takes a lot more time. You think you're whispering when you're really shouting. That is one of the most difficult things.

The most exciting time in my life as a father is now— when they're entering puberty and adolescence, because they talk back and they're very articulate and sensitive. And I like that; they'll tell me I'm full of shit or whatever, and we can talk about it. Of course, the acting-out part of being teenagers and being able to articulate certain perspectives I can do without, but it's when we break through and we actually sit down that they teach me far more than I ever taught them. This is the time when I am actually forced to negotiate my power as father in an important way. If I am too lenient, they don't see strength and commitment on my part; yet, on the other hand, if I am too rigid, they will feel oppressed.

Part of the challenge is that I still haven't learned how to accept the kind of unqualified love that my children bring to me. To increase the feeling that I deserve their unqualified love requires a certain kind of trust. My wife and I have different roles in our family. One of my roles is to be the enforcer. So, they'll be storming the gates, on one hand, because I'm the Gatekeeper. But on the other hand, I have to allow for that and still be stern, all the while hoping that they divorce that from the person they know me really to be.

At the beginning, parenting is simpler. You say things like, "You can't touch the stove because it's hot," because you can't let them burn their hand. When they get older, however, it becomes much more complex. Like curfew. Or clothing. "You can't have the seventy-five-dollar pair of jeans." "No, I don't think that bathing suit is appropriate." All that kind of stuff is a lot more complicated than "Don't touch the stove." Also, just learning how to provide for someone else's needs is difficult because you have to provide for them at the same time you are teaching them to provide for themselves. How do you really reinforce their sense of self at all times? It's easy to say I love you every day. You wake up. You keep telling your daughter you love her, that she's beautiful. But that ain't it. It's far more complicated than that. It's your example —how you live every day, how much time you're there, your level of tolerance and how well you listen. What do you do if your world has collapsed that day? You come home, drink a half bottle of wine and you go to bed? It's complicated.

Then too, your children's unqualified love means they can also inflict pain on you. I think every child is always astonished when they realize for the first time that they might be able to beat their father in arm wrestling, but they can demolish you emotionally when they acquire linguistic skills. Our house is not "Ho, ho, Daddy, welcome home, and here's your pipe and slippers." Five years ago, when we had just moved to Massachusetts, we were arguing one time, and Maggie said, "What difference does it make to you? You don't live here anyway." I was hurt! I can joke about it now, but it was not funny—I was devastated. Learning to take advice, getting over pain, this is the hardest lesson—getting over your anger and your pain. And then learning a lesson from it. And then repairing the situation. That is the process of fatherhood. That is it. These are the steps: anger, healing, lesson, prevention. And then not repeating, not getting in cycles. And then trying not to perpetuate your own kind of madnesses on your kids.

So, I learn from raising my daughters. But I also want them to learn from me. I want them to learn how to trust themselves because they are brilliant and beautiful and they have enormous integrity. I want them to trust themselves and to know that they can excel—they really can. No matter how much self-doubt they may feel being black in America, I want them to know that they have to resist doubt and know that they are a superior people. Everybody's not created equal as far as I'm concerned. I mean, in some broad sense before the law, they are, but not in terms of endowment. My kids are marvelously endowed.

Another lesson that I want my kids to learn from me is illustrated in this story. A man walked by another old man who's a great fisherman—he had all these fish on his line. They had both been fishing the same amount of time. One guy had nothing—he had not even gotten a bite. He asked the other man, "What's your secret—how did you catch all these fish?" And the man looked at him and said, " 'Cause I keep my pole in the water all the time." My message to them is: keep your pole in the water all the time. If it doesn't work this way, try that way. Confront the thing that you're most afraid of because you'll have this great sense of triumph. I think that life is about work and about pleasure. I think you should play hard, you should work hard, and you shouldn't confuse them. In the end, you have to please no one but yourself.

I try to show my children that they should try not to be swayed by the crowd. I've seen people at political rallies stand up and say all kinds of weird things, and they get standing ovations. Yet all around you people are whispering, "Did you actually believe that?" "No, I didn't believe that bullshit." And yet the need to be accepted causes them to do things contrary to their own instincts, their own integrity, their own best self-interest. Whether it's with a lover or with a group, whether it's political or whether it's personal, you can't be loved and you can't be respected unless you respect and love yourself. That would be my bottom line for my daughters. Even if everybody else turns against them, their mother and I will still be there.

My father also taught me wonderful lessons that I want to pass on to my children. One was: I can always come home. I remember when I was going off to Yale, the last thing my father said to me was, "If you get up there and they don't treat you right, or if you get up there and you're not happy, you can always come home and it won't matter." He meant it. Sometimes you say something like, "I pledge allegiance to the flag," and it has no weight. But when you tell somebody you really love them, and they hear it, it's like beauty to the ears. My father said that to me in a way that made me feel free. If I had to identify one thing that was responsible for my success as an undergraduate, it was the freedom to fail. I knew that my parents would never turn against me, no matter what I did, and I would want my daughters to feel the same way.

The second critical thing I got from my father was this: once I said to him, "Johnny Dipilato told me, 'Dutch Boggs gets a dollar for every A on his report card.' " I always got straight A's, so I said, "I want to get a dollar, too." My father said, "No way, you shouldn't work for that." So I said, "Well, what would you do if I got an F?" My father replied, "If you goofed off and got an F, I'd be pissed off. If you did your best and got an F, that's the best you could do." Then he added, "But if you did your best, you wouldn't get an F." It's a paradox, but he was right. But somehow there's a liberating element in that paradox—you're free. I got straight A's.

The funny thing is, being a father helps me understand my father much differently. It makes me sympathize with difficult choices he had to make, which I didn't understand. I like the way he clearly loves my children, unambivalently. So whatever ambivalence he and I might have had, which was considerable, particularly when I was at the same age my kids are now, he has none with them. Someone once said that the reason grandparents and grandchildren get on so well is that they have a common enemy. So being a parent makes me like him more. You know, even if I get mad at him, I say, well, at least he loves my children—his grandchildren, and that's good.

The main thing a parent must remember is that a child is a human being who has feelings and desires and passions and pain; as a parent, you're an agent in affecting all those things. Learning that and trying to be a person who's worthy of all this love that they're so willing to give you is a very difficult task. The paradox of being a parent is that at birth, you have the maximum amount of love you can have from the child. Then you only lose it. You can never get more than you have in all that innocence when you are the maximum provider. The more they get to know you, the more qualified their love becomes. And your goal, your challenge, is to be aware of the dangers of that process—the necessity of it, but also the dangers of it. Then to do as much as you can to check it, do as much as you can to earn the innocence of the love that they gave you from the time that they were born. That is an awesome, awesome burden.

Playthell Benjamin

Reflections on Fatherhood

Playthell Benjamin is a contributing editor at Emerge *magazine, an op-ed columnist for the* New York Daily News, *and a regular contributor to the* Village Voice, *the* Times *of* London, *and the* Manchester Guardian. *He lectures widely on music, politics, and race.*

Song for My Father

Sorry I didn't get to know you
I guess you just checked out too soon
But I know you musta been a real hip cat
'Cause you ended up pulling the Queen
Sometimes I wish there really was a heaven out there
Where good folks go when they die
'Cause I know one day I'd run into you somewhere
Blowin' soul and decked out fly
The old Folks say you had the gift of gab
And I know I talk mucho shit!
So even tho' I didn't get to know you
Seems heredity sure did its bit
I hear tell you was a coal black, double cool,
Zoot suit-wearing cat
And Mom's a foxy high brown Queen
Now, I know y'all musta did it to death
Like Ellington's fantasy
In Black and Tan
I know, 'cause I done seen y'all strollin'
In the cinema of my mind

A s Wole Soyinka once said of his father, my daddy, George "Chermopolese" Benjamin, "danced and
joined the ancestors" when I was only four years old.
Hence, fate denied me the opportunity to know him. The
actual memories I hold of my father are faded impres-
sions of a dark-skinned man dressed in a white gown
sitting in a wheelchair in the visiting rooms of Jefferson
Hospital, the distinguished teaching hospital of the University of Pennsylvania, where I was born and where my
mother later took me to receive therapy for a considerable
speech impediment that reduced me to a sweat, and almost to tears whenever I attempted to speak—a condition
so long past that I barely remember it. My only memory
of my father outside the hospital is a stern voice at the
dinner table admonishing me: "You, boy! When you've
got to scrape your plate, you're through eating." Virtually
all that I know of my father I have learned through the
revelations of others, and many people have contributed
bits and pieces to the puzzle. From the picture that has
emerged he was quite an admirable fellow.

I became aware early on of my father's reputation as a
real dap dude, a paragon of male elegance, from the com-

ments of my sixth-grade math teacher, Mrs. Mills, a jock
fox who was light/bright/damn near white and who had
also taught my father. She would greet me at the classroom door with a smile as warm and bright as the Florida
sunshine and declare with much fanfare: "You sure look
sharp today! You remind me of your father; George always looked like he'd just stepped out of a band box."
This was before I broke free of my mother's sartorial tyr-
anny and started wearing dungarees and khaki pants to
school. In those days my mother chose my outfits and
imposed my father's—and her own—standards in attire.
A fashion plate in her own right, Moms, who is the
daughter of a splendid seamstress and always had her
clothes custom-made, would later introduce me to tai-
lored suits, an acquired taste that I retained for many
years.

Then one day I noticed the source of all the fuss: an
eight-by-ten photograph of "Daddy George" that my
grandfather, George Benjamin, Sr., kept on the coffee table in his living room. It was a full-length shot of my
father dressed to the nines in a suit, tie, and one of those
broad-brim Stetson skys that were so popular in the for-
ties. The picture made the point: Pops was as clean as the
board of health! And a picture of me in a yellow play suit
with large white collar, taken when I won a baby contest
at eleven months old, still sits atop my mother's mantel
in a gilded double picture frame that I share with my
sister, Melba, who looks like a cuddly brown doll with
bright eyes that mirror the wonder of the brand-new
world about her. We were living testaments to my parents' intention to pass on their high style and fine sartorial taste to us.

But what my mother mostly talked about where my father was concerned was how he adored his family. Theirs was a great love story that ended in tragedy far too soon. They were high school sweethearts who eloped after graduation because my maternal grandfather wouldn't give his permission to marry. And that was no small consideration because Walter "Big Nang" Bellamy was a formidable adversary. People said he looked like Joe Louis, except he was a lot bigger. He was a legendary character who treasured books; could break a horse or a bully; grow tomatoes the size of cantaloupes; top off the biggest steel structure in town with hot rivets; lead a swinging jazz band; play the ivory off the piano keys in ragtime or classical sonata; lift his piano on the back of his truck by his lonesome; went off to fight the kaiser in Europe and came back with battle ribbons; slapped the cracker sheriff of Saint John's County with his hand wide open and put the ill-mannered peckerwood in a coma for three days; lived to bullshit about it later, and now takes his rest in an elegant white soldiers grave in the national cemetery along the beautiful Matanzas Bay, about a mile or so from the Fountain of Youth in Saint Augustine.

"Big Nang" wanted his daughters to get a college education—like his sisters, my grand aunts Marie and Rosa. My mother's sisters, Rosalie and Margaret, both earned college degrees, but my mother marched to my daddy's rhythm. Instead of getting off the train in Washington, where Moms was to attend Howard University, she stayed on board and traveled to Philadelphia, in a rare act of defiance of her father, a man whom she held in such esteem she once told me: "If my daddy told me the sun wasn't coming up the next morning, I would have gone to sleep prepared to wake up in the dark." In Philadelphia she and my daddy were married. But after a few years of what, from my mother's description, sounds like marital bliss, my daddy took sick and died. My mother was twenty-two and my father twenty-five. His passing was all the more traumatic for my mother because he was a robust and energetic man.

I am still amazed at Dad's industry, sobriety, and sense of responsibility. In his early twenties in apartheid America, he was, amazingly, buying a house while supporting a wife and two children. His work ethic was astonishing. During the day he was a welder at Sun Shipyard in nearby Chester, Pennsylvania—the same shipyard where Brent Staples tells us his father worked during the period of "industrial prosperity" in his moving memoir *Parallel Lives*, and at night Pops attended classes in heating and refrigeration. Then, on weekends, he cut hair in a barber shop he had set up in the basement of our South Philly home. Yet after all of that, my mother could still say: "Every time your daddy looked at me, I felt like I was about to get pregnant again."

Aside from stories about how hard he worked and what a wonderful, loving husband he was, my mother never tired of telling us how my father's favorite recreation was to push me and my sister, Melba, around our largely Italian neighborhood in a tandem carriage on his evenings off—after she had groomed and decorated us to perfection. The highest compliment Moms can pay me as a parent is to say: "You remind me of your daddy with those kids. That man acted like he thought you all were the most precious children in the world." Although I cannot remember my father well enough to recall his love and kindness, I have a good idea what it was like because I was pampered and treated like a prince by everyone in my family, including my many uncles, a group of tradesmen and small businessmen who were wedded to the Protestant work ethic and were prosperous home owners whom I never saw idle or unemployed a day in my life. It was my uncles who told me more than a few of the stories about my father that helped shape the conception of him that I hold today. I was lucky, I never had to search for role models.

My uncle Jimmy, a brilliant and elegant man with a stuttering problem, was fascinated with my pop's gift of gab and often told me stories of his glib tongue and irreverent wit. One story he loved to tell was how they were kicked out of school for a stint during senior year for performing a comic skit in assembly that was conceived by my father. "I didn't really know what George had in mind when he asked me to do it. All he told me was, 'Now, Jimmy, every time I ask you a question, just answer rubber.' Well, that's all I did too, but it got me in a world of trouble. The question was: 'What stretches the farthest, skin or rubber?' I said rubber, and he asked, 'Are you sure? Well what does the Bible say: skin or rubber?' And once more I said, 'rubber.' Then George pulled out the Bible and read this passage that said Jesus tied his ass to a tree and walked from Jerusalem to Galilee! Then he asked: 'Now, tell me some rubber that can stretch that far.' But the principal didn't think it was so funny. We were tossed out on our behinds for a few days, and our parents had to come to the school for a meeting."

Then there were other stories about Dad's athletic prowess as a swimmer and tennis player. My favorite swimming story was one I heard my grandfather tell over and over again during my childhood. He would gaze out over the Saint Johns River and say, "Boy, your daddy was the most famous swimmer in town. Why, he could dive off the docks with the Bible in his hand, then float all the way over to the other bank lying on his back reading the scripture and never get the Bible wet!" And he seems to have been something of a tennis hustler too, since he lived next door to the courts and could take anybody on any given day.

What fascinates me most about these stories today is that the range of activities he engaged in suggests that my father's generation had broader interests than are associated with working-class black men today, when activities like tennis and swimming are viewed as the province of middle-class whites. Indeed, this limited view of the range of interests appropriate to African-American males has extended to all classes. When various commentators, black and white, wanted to make the point that O. J. Simpson was "too white" in his behavior, they invariably pointed to the fact that he plays golf. But all of my uncles played golf sixty years ago, and they were hardly around whites at all, especially in a social capacity. When my father was coming of age, there was a widespread belief in the power of education, and it was an article of faith that education, skill, and personal achievement were the only valid measures of a man. So the trick to getting ahead in life was to get as much education as possible, then work like hell! Hence, they refused to believe that anything which was a part of the human heritage was beyond their grasp.

My father's belief in advanced notions like the universality of human experience was demonstrated in his addition of a middle name, an act that also testifies to his grand conception of himself. Concluding that George Benjamin was too common a name for his unique character, he decided, after copping a new wardrobe with some of his C.C. camp money, that he would hire a lawyer to file the necessary papers officially adding a middle name of his invention: "Chermopolese." I imagine he was attracted to it because it has a certain grandeur that conjures up the spirit of ancient Greece. Remember, this was before the widespread reclamation of ancient Egypt as the cradle of the black civilization.

I have forgiven him for this Eurocentric twist and chosen to regard it as further evidence of an attitude that allowed him the freedom to dream grandiose dreams and envision himself in roles that black boys living under the restrictions of a white supremacist caste society were not supposed to covet. And I thank him over and over in absentia for deciding that I would grow up to become a unique personality and inventing a unique name for me: Playthell. For, according to my mother, the real Queen Elizabeth, that's how I got it. And although my name was a source of embarrassment among my peers when I was growing up, I learned to love it as a young adult after I discovered that it was an instant conversation piece when I was introduced to the ladies.

My father's cosmopolitan approach to life was promoted by the teachers at Excelsior, the little brick school that served the African-American community and accounts for the fact that the little black community in Saint Augustine,

Florida, produced an unusually large percentage of officers in the armed forces during World War II. While my daddy stayed on the homefront and worked in the war production industry, Uncle Jimmy became a combat officer. As I grew older he also became my role model. Although he had a son and three daughters, we managed a relationship that was quite special. When it came to fathering, Uncle Jimmy seemed born to the role. After he and my aunt Juanita raised their own brood, they raised several children of relatives and friends who had died or fallen on hard times. His elegant style and manners, work ethic and high-minded values, personified the things my father stood for and, along with his many stories about my dad, provided me a vicarious experience with him.

Along with Uncle Jimmy—whom I saw only sporadically when I was growing up because he lived in New York and my mother moved back to the beautiful peaceful little town of Saint Augustine—there were many other men in my life, including my grandfather and my uncles Walter, Irvin, Buddy, and Bill. All of them had some pretty fascinating stories to tell in their own right. They all spent time with me and told me stories about my pops. So, in spite of the fact that I spent my formative years in a single-parent, female-headed household, I had little in common with the multitude of angry young black men who are wreaking havoc in the African-American community today. I am convinced that the anger and nihilism expressed by these young men is rooted in their abandonment by their fathers. This connection is most evident in their contempt for adult male authority, especially black adults. The big difference between me and them is that I always knew that my father was an honorable man who loved us.

I cannot even begin to imagine what it must be like to be told by your mother: "Your father ain't shit!" But many of these young men who casually commit murder and mayhem have heard their mothers say this countless times. Oftentimes they live in communities where nuclear families are rare and their mothers socialize with other women who have been abandoned by their children's father, and it becomes commonplace to hear the broader indictment: "Nigger men ain't shit!" Hence it is not surprising that many of these young men attempt to build self-esteem through misogyny and murder. All one need do to recognize these connections is to listen to the rappers and study the family profiles of the young men who are arrested for murder and other vicious acts that provide a false sense of power.

The failure of young black men and women to behave responsibly in the area of reproduction and child rearing represents a menace to the stability of black America unlike anything we have yet experienced. According to the studies of Herbert Gutman and others, the black nuclear family was stronger under slavery. Therefore, attempts to blame the fact that seventy percent of black births occurring out of wedlock in 1994 to the experience of slavery is transparent nonsense. This problem is the result of forces of recent origin; it is the reflection of an economic crisis as well as a crisis of values.

African-American sociologist William Julius Wilson has documented the devastating effect on black community life that has resulted from the explosion of single-parent, female-headed impoverished households, and demonstrated its relationship to the permanent economic crisis growing out of radical changes in the urban economy that make assuming the roles of husband and father an unrealistic option for many young working-class black males who are structurally unemployed or working for subsistence wages.

As a father with two teenage high school children, I am acutely aware of how much things have changed since I entered high school in 1955. It was, to say the least, a different world. To begin with, most black children in America will attend schools that are as segregated as the schools I attended in Florida before the *Brown* decision. The difference is that these schools are in too many instances run by whites—either as principals or school superintendents—who for the most part know nothing of the history and culture of the students they serve. Hence today's black students do not have the benefit of teachers who have a visceral connection to and can introduce the students to the existential richness of the songs, stories, history, and literature of African-Americans that provided inspiration to the students of my generation. Nor will they have the benefit of the teachers themselves as role models.

If they attend predominately white suburban schools, they could well spend their school days feeling alienated from their classmates, as W. E. B. Du Bois describes in *Dusk of Dawn*, or as the spate of books written by students who went through the ABC program in the 1960s and 1970s so painfully recount. Yet even this alienated existence begins to look good when compared to the dangerous conditions of many predominately black inner-city schools. For instance, there were five hundred robberies in New York City's public schools in the first six months of the 1994-95 school year, and stories of random murder and mayhem are so commonplace in black communities from coast to coast that black-on-black homicide has become the main cause of death among young African-American males. The question that I continually ask is: Why is it that my children face dangers from their fellow black brothers and sisters that never crossed my mind when I was their age forty years ago? Not only did I not fear serious bodily harm from other black youths, but I felt no imminent danger from whites either. I was wary of them and knew that they could be dangerous, but I did not fear them the way my children fear the criminal violence among their African-American peers today. At least we knew what to expect from southern whites—and most of us knew intuitively how to deal with that.

But the violence among today's black youth is so often senseless, without rhyme or reason, that it smacks of a growing epidemic of self-destructiveness. And, like many parents, I am not sure what to do about it, what's the best advice to give my children about the best way to protect themselves. I believe the answer to this sad enigma lies in finding ways to compensate for the breakdown of the African-American family resulting from out-of-wedlock births and the wholesale abandonment of children by a growing segment of the black male population. This question is usually greeted with the overworked cliché "It takes a whole village to raise a child," but the problem is too widespread and there is no institutional structure to deal with it. The church is providing heroic service, but their resources are limited and they are being over-whelmed.

In an attempt to embarrass young men into behaving more responsibly, Reverend Jesse Jackson is fond of say-ing: "Even a dog will raise his pups." But that is only partially true. The female will raise the pups, but the males walk. While this behavior may work for dogs, as a program for human development it has proven disas-trous. Even as I write this essay, *NBC Dateline* is airing yet another program profiling the lives of a group of dead-end kids from Bedford Stuyvesant in Brooklyn, New York. We first encounter these kids in the fourth grade, then check them out later in life after most of the boys have dropped out of school, turned to selling drugs, and accumulated criminal records.

The missing father and struggling mother is a persis-tent theme in the lives of these black and Puerto Rican boys. According to this program, the girls fared better. Eight out of ten of those who went on to college were girls, while all of those who went to jail were boys. One of the girls graduated from college with honors in three years. Lamentations about absentee fathers laced the nar-ratives of all these young people, and many attributed the success rate of the females to the examples set by their mothers and grandmothers. Ironically, five of the males in the class have fathered children out of wedlock.

When I was twenty years old, I too fathered a child out of wedlock. Having been raised in a community where one was expected to "do the right thing" if one got a girl "in trouble," I was prepared to marry. But I was a radical activist in the movement, and the young woman was apo-litical. When we were only dating, that was not much of a problem, but when we started contemplating a life together it became a major obstacle. I was advised against marriage by my closest political comrades, which included women, one of whom offered to adopt the child if the pregnant woman wanted to continue her life without the responsibility of a child. I would hear none of it and was determined to get married anyway. In the end, however, our constant bickering about politics led to the unraveling of the relationship, and she left me before my first child, a daughter, was born, and moved a thousand miles away. Shortly after my daughter's birth her mother married, and I saw my daughter only sporadically over the years. Fortunately, we have a fine relationship today, but I believe the absence of a normal relationship earlier in her life was damaging, and I regret that she had to pay a price for events over which she had no control.

I was determined that this would never happen to another child of mine, and I pledged to be the best father possible the second time around. Part of that pledge had to do with making sure that I produced no more children out of wedlock, a commitment that I managed to keep in spite of the fact that I was single for a considerable part of my adult life. When my twins, Makeda and Samori, were born, my wife, June, and I had been married for several years. Since I had decided to pursue a career as a writer in my late thirties, I was uninterested in assuming the responsibility of fatherhood. But June had other ideas. Like myself, she had also lost a parent at four years old, but she had lost her mother and longed for a mother-child experience. Being the strong-willed, independent-minded woman that she is, June decided that we would have a child and ditched her contraceptives without in-

forming me. Hence in a moment of unguarded passion
while we were away on a holiday, the miracle of conception occurred and, to my astonishment, we were the
proud parents of twins seven and a half months later. It
was strange the way it all happened.

At first I thought of trying to persuade my wife to have
an abortion. I was pushing forty, my coin was in limited
supply, and I was embarking on a writing career as I
approached middle age that a baby would surely cause
me to put on hold. But after viewing sonograms that revealed we were having twins, the idea of abortion became
hideous to me, and I played past the whole thing. It
would not have mattered anyway because there was no
way that June was going for it! And for the record, it was
the worst idea I ever had, because Makeda and Samori
are the best things that ever happened to me, even though
I had to put my writing career on hold for several years.

It was after a visit with Uncle Jimmy, who was into
the process of realizing his dream of owning a first-class
New York restaurant, that I began to look optimistically
upon a second chance at fatherhood. The day we talked,
I had gone over to Brooklyn Heights, an elegant and
super-affluent bedroom community in downtown Brooklyn, where several men in the family were busy transforming a stately nineteenth-century bank building into
the Ferry Bank Restaurant under the direction of Jimmy
Jr., Uncle Jimmy's son, who is a fine architect and a splendid father of two sons himself. Uncle Jimmy explained
that he and Aunt Nita had been living in such cramped
quarters when their second child, cousin Joanie, was born
that they made her a crib in the dresser drawer. He could
not understand how I could even contemplate such a

thing as an abortion when my wife had no children and yearned to be a mother. Plus, he pointed out that I had plenty of space for children, living as I was in Paul Robeson's old Sugar Hill apartment.

The night my children were born, my wife and I were watching *Black Power in the Ring*, a documentary on Jack Johnson, the first black heavyweight champion of the world. I was enthralled with the old black-and-white film clips showing J.J. busting white boys' asses and getting paid, when June suddenly went into labor. Since it was seven weeks to her delivery date, neither of us thought the children were on the way. I had spent weeks in classes learning how to assist my wife during delivery, but the process went so fast I never got a chance to employ my skills. In about two hours from the first stab of pain, I was the father of two children. When I first saw them, I was shocked and immediately started to worry.

They seemed so small! My son weighed four and a half pounds, and his twin sister, who was his senior by three and a half minutes, weighed only four. But it was not their size alone that disturbed me; it was what seemed like an endless tangle of plastic tubes attached to their veins, intravenously feeding fluids into their bodies. For a moment I wondered if they were going to make it, and my anxiety was soothed only after a doctor on the delivery team noticed my panic and took me over to the incubator and showed me a baby born to a dope-fiend mother. The baby weighed one and a half pounds and was plagued with a host of drug-induced problems. After I peeped that kid's story, I was all right. I was convinced that my kids were going to be cool.

Because the babies showed on the scene so far ahead

of their estimated time of arrival, nothing was ready to receive them. Their cribs were still in the boxes, and their nursery room was unpainted. In spite of the early arrival, Mom's jaws got tight when she and my sisters Melba and Claudia drove up the next day and found me frantically painting. But before the day was over everything was in order, thanks to fast-drying latex paint and the many hands that pitched in to make the work easier. In spite of the conceits of the downtown crowd, Harlem has some of the finest town houses and apartments in the city, especially in the Sugar Hill section. Before the day was over, the room was converted into one of the loveliest nurseries in town; I'd bet my bottom dollar on it. Painted in bright pink and green colors, the room had everything: lace curtains, lovely throw rugs, state-of-the-art cribs, a large dressing table with miniature bathtubs and mono-grammed towels, and complex mobiles hanging from the thirteen-feet ceilings. It was fit for a little prince and princess—which is how everybody on both sides of the family has treated them ever since. Many of the various items were gifts from family members, so it hardly cost us a dime.

It was a good thing too, because when the children came on October 1, 1981, my money was tight. At the time June became pregnant, she was working as an assistant to the director of nursing at Columbia Presbyterian Hospital, where the babies were born, so the delivery was covered by her job. For the last few years I had been in the music business: writing lyrics to original tunes by composers, playing drums, managing a band, and trying to produce a record independently—an activity that led to bankruptcy. I was trying to establish an income as a freelance writer, and I was scared to death that I might not be able to put bread on the table. After all, with two babies to care for, it would be a while before June could return to work, and I felt inadequate enough watching her nurse both the babies from her breasts at once. So along with the arrival of the babies came a great deal of pressure.

I remembered how my uncle Buddy had clomped around the house in his work boots, holding my cousin T in his arms when Auntie Margaret brought him home from the hospital, swearing that although he was just a working man without much education, he would find a way to give his son the American dream. And he did too. With a loan from my mother—who had received a tidy sum from my daddy's life insurance benefits after suing Tennessee National Insurance Company, who tried to beat her—Uncle Buddy and his brother Bill bought the trucking company they were working for. Their example boosted my confidence that I would find a way to meet my responsibilities as a father too. With that faith, I donned my thinking cap and stepped to it. The first thing I did was to start figuring out if it was possible to support a family from writing. Since I had no track record as a writer I had my doubts, and I was prepared to give up the whole enterprise. That's why I didn't want to assume the responsibility of fatherhood. Never having known a man in my family who had not risen to the occasion, I was terrified at the possibility of being the first to fail.

It didn't take long to see that we would starve if I spent my time writing the sort of weighty treatises I had in mind. So I went to work at various jobs—one of them was as a boxing publicist, another was as a construction worker. But, most important, I always made it possible to be with my babies. From the very beginning I took an active part in their upbringing, routinely rising early in the morning to bathe and dress them, then take them to their mother for the first feeding of the day. We shared many sublime moments, and they learned to say, "Dada" the first words out of their little mouths, much to my wife's chagrin.

As they grew older and June reentered the work force, we hired a wonderful grandmother, a retired civil servant, to care for them. When the weather was nice, we gave her carfare to take the children to the playgrounds at the Metropolitan Museum of Art, on Fifth Avenue, where all the rich white kids play. This was the beginning of our effort to instill the idea in them that they were New Yorkers and every public space in the city belonged as much to them as anyone else. Hence today, at fourteen years old, Makeda and Samori think of themselves as New Yorkers, not ghetto dwellers, in spite of the fact that they were born and raised in Harlem. Occasionally, she would bring them by the construction site when I was working near parks, and I would spend my lunch break with the children. Seeing them always gave me a lift, and the balance of the day breezed by. The construction industry was a racist cesspool where black and Hispanic men had to literally fight for a piece of the action, and having the babies gave me strength for the fight. The experience provided me invaluable insights into the plight of the black working man in his struggle for bread.

The realities of racial exclusion in the construction business made writing for a living look more and more attractive. So during one of my frequent layoffs I started writing in earnest, and I've been writing ever since.

Like many parents of my generation who struggled in the sixties, I thought my children would be spared the racial battles we faced. But we overlooked the fact that racist repression is a cyclical phenomenon, and it appears that we are facing a downturn in the quest for racial equality. What then is the role of the African-American father in these troubled times? The first step is to plan when to become a father. This means establishing an economic foundation that can support a family in a reasonably comfortable lifestyle, because it is clear that poverty damages our children in a variety of ways. It also means that you plan to be there for the long haul; be a responsible adult and do not walk away as soon as you no longer feel fulfilled by your marriage. Since fatherless black children have become a cliché, to abandon one's children is to stigmatize them, and our children will have enough stigmas to bear just being born black in America. Furthermore, a wealth of data shows that children with both parents enjoy greater economic and emotional security.

A good father must spend time with his children, sometimes doing what they want and other times doing things that he deems important. I have often noticed the paucity of black parents, and black fathers in particular, escorting their children to the great museums and art galleries that are so pervasive in the big cities of this nation. These kind of activities enrich the relationship between parent and child while contributing to their intellectual growth. This is of fundamental importance. We must set high standards for intellectual and other worthwhile endeavors and insist that our children strive for excellence, not because their success or failure reflects on our self-esteem, but as a way of teaching them to aim high and that their reach should exceed their grasp. And we must not be shy about telling our children that we love them and expressing it physically by hugging and kissing.

Tell your children that racism and discrimination is a reflection of white folks' fear of fair and open competition with us. Explain that it wasn't long ago that white men swore that no black man possessed the skill and courage necessary to win the heavyweight championship in the boxing ring, the finesse to play in the NBA, or the intelligence to play quarterback or manage a baseball team. Then point out that they should give no more weight to white folks' claims to intellectual superiority than their former claims to athletic supremacy. Inundate your children with videotapes, newspapers, and magazine articles about outstanding black people wherever they are. Give high priority to taking them to see great black performers in the theater and concerts. I believe that once our children experience the magic and majesty of great black performers, it is impossible to convince them that they belong to an inferior people. And, in this regard, teach them about our heroic struggle against white oppression by buying them books on our history: fiction and nonfiction. But most of all, we must convey to them that true self-esteem comes from individual accomplishment! So teach them to be prepared when they go to class and speak up; don't take a backseat to anyone.

I also think it is critical to impress upon our children at an early age that being black in America doesn't have to be a drag. One of the ways I address this problem is simply to ask my son to try to imagine what it must be like to be Colin Powell, Wynton Marsalis, Michael Jordan, Jesse Jackson, David Dinkins, Reginald Lewis, Denzel Washington, or a host of writers, scholars, scientists, artists, and businessmen that we know. I ask my daughter the same question: what does it require to be Dr. Mae Jamison, Toni Morrison, Carol Moseley Braun, Elaine Jones, Anna Deveare Smith, Kathleen Battle, Eleanor Holmes Norton, FloJo, Cassandra Wilson, Nancy Wilson, et al? And, of course, there is the constant example of their mother and me nearby, along with a host of strong, intelligent men and women in our family.

The point of all this is to stress the fact that in spite of persistent obstacles, excellence in any worthwhile endeavor will eventually be rewarded. But I also strive to demonstrate the truth of the old adage "Excellence is its own reward." Since we are dealing with human beings, who are very complex and unpredictable creatures, there are no foolproof formulas for success. But thus far I've got two delightful teenagers who are self-confident and full of optimism about the future. My daughter tells that she intends to become first a lawyer, then a congresswoman, then the first black woman president of the United States! After all this she intends to write fiction on the side. And she's the kind of kid who has the intelligence, drive, and self-confidence to pull it off too. Hence I make no attempt to temper her ambition by warning her to watch out for glass ceilings, although I know they are firmly in place. And after reading books like Ellis Cose's *The Rage of a Privileged Class*, I sometimes wonder if I'm doing the right thing.

I do talk to my children about racism in general, however, but since they have never really experienced it in any concrete form, it is a fairly abstract concept to them. Still, like most thoughtful African-American parents, I am torn between the fear of thwarting their ambitions by telling them all I know about the realities of race in America, and risking the possibility of leaving them psychologically unprepared to deal with the white racist behavior they are certain to experience sooner or later. I am especially concerned about my son. By virtue of his good looks, charming personality, general intelligence, and athletic ability I worry less about how he will deal with white racism than the dangers he faces from his black and Hispanic peers. It's sad but true. The fact that my boy is a really mellow kid, who would rather listen to sports radio and Wynton Marsalis than gangster rappers, means that he could be marked as "soft" by some of the wannabe gangstas roaming the streets and subways of New York.

Still in all, the most revolutionary thing a black man can do at this point in our history is marry a black woman and raise some children. In other words, somebody ought to tell these brothers who are running around spouting revolutionary rhetoric while making babies all over the place, a serious commitment to fatherhood is our greatest obligation and our highest calling in service to the African-American nation. Plus, beyond all the political jazz, playing the role of father has been the greatest joy of my life.

Robert G. O'Meally

Of Sons and Fathers: Remembering George M. O'Meally

Robert G. O'Meally is a professor of English and Comparative Literature at Columbia University. He is the author of Lady Day: The Many Faces of Billie Holliday *and* History and Memory in African American Culture *and has published many articles on Ralph Ellison, jazz, and African-American literature.*

This is a story about fathering and about my father, George M. O'Meally, who died when I was nineteen turning twenty, and whom I loved. It is a tale of a father by a son who is now himself a father, by one whose memory is full of enchantment, and who witnesses the world through a veil of the sweet thunder music and cadenced speech from long-gone yesteryears, none of whose sounds reverberates more clearly in my head than does the voice of my father speaking to me.

I'll tell about him by telling about another of my fathers, and about a scene and a time that sparked my memory and ignited my myth-making imagination. It was a story colliding with other stories, a tale of percussion and repercussion.

My son Gabriel was seven then, and had never before visited the Harlem home of my friend the writer Albert Murray. This was by intention and design, for Mister Murray had told me years before I had children of my own how it burned him when people brought kids to his Lenox Terrace apartment (Harlem's finest), with its Beardens hanging low and its first editions standing tall in fine dust-jacketed elegance on the long book boards that covered one wall.

He cut short all such visits, he told me then, with his deep Louis Armstrong laugh, by making the parents feel at least as nervous as he was about the expensive things all around the apartment. Every time Junior leaned or even looked in the wrong direction, Mister Murray would start up and inhale a warning whistle until Papa and Mama put Trouble out of doors again and peace was at last restored.

This was not, please understand, because Mister Murray disliked kids, particularly. After all, he had a daughter of his own, Michele, now grown, and he still doted on her. And in Murray's novels his kids shine with possibility that is the envy of most of the adults, who generally appear not as heroes of the future (if heroes they be at all) but of the past: retired pathfinders full of shade-tree encouragements and examples and cautionary tales told with a wink. Murray's top hero-children, inevitably based on recollections of his own first days, were boxcar jumpers, secret adventurers of the outback, dragon slayers in training. Scooter, the main man of *Train-Whistle Guitar*, is that book's Jack the Rabbit, Jack the Bear, a bad Buster Brownskin on his way somewhere: the Young Man with a plan.

So when it came to curious kids with high energy, Murray knew precisely who it was that he was scaring out of the cabbage patch, which in this case was lined with rare arugulas and special tender endives along with a few make-believe sunflowers and snapdragons and perhaps an origami paper frog or two. I mean, Murray's apartment was a writer's dream place, a high-perch urban chinaberry tree with a view that inspired stories and expert ways of telling them. Even so, I felt that Gabe, my rough and tumble second son, was ready.

"So, Gabe," I said to him as we turned from the sidewalk into Lenox Terrace. "At the Murrays' place, behave yourself, man! Act the way you do when you visit Nonny and Poppy" (his strict-on-manners grandparents in Virginia). He looked back at me with his special Bogart-movie squint, sizing me up and ready to make a deal.

The visit itself I remember as a series of dynamic images and subtly pitched sound patterns. There was the summertime tinkling chill of the glasses of fresh iced tea; the delicate beauty of Mrs. Murray's down-home song-speech (now high and clear: "Well, Gabriel, look how big you are!" now whispery low and conspiratorial: "I bet you'd like to help me see about some cookies? You come with me"); Mister Murray seeing Gabe play with his artist's movable wooden figure of a human form and telling him, "Yeess, go on son: take it down, have a closer look"; Gabe's guilty-thief joyous looks in my direction.

Mister Murray knew Gabe by reputation, and seemed to sparkle as he watched the boy moving around the rooms in a slow-motion waltz, a prizefighter in a parlor, doing his best not to draw any lightning bolts from Daddy. It was Mister Murray who had not flinched at all when I told him about Gabe's brushes with authorities in school, due mainly to a tendency to throw his hands before he'd given words much of a fighting chance. The most recent incident had won the boy his first (not his last) lecture in the principal's office.

"You must see a red light in your head, and stop yourself from going too far," she had told him, again. Both Gabe and I stared back at her, Gabe looking like the last boy in town to feel penitent. Yes, he'd done it, his face said. So what? Behind that mask he was a little sorry—at least he was sorry about all the fuss that was being kicked up—but he was not going to give in and outright apologize. He looked like a little criminal, and my heart was not easy.

During that season of worry Murray told me: "Yeah, well, that's where he's supposed to be—in trouble. He's got energy and imagination, and he's testing himself and everybody else, including you! He's got to find some trouble that way. And remember, Bob, he's going to have something I bet you did not have at his age. He actually knows already what it is that trouble looks like. That can do him good later on. And he knows something about adult disapproval, too, that you perhaps never knew first-hand. I bet you were never down in the principal's office for anything but some kind of jivetime prize or hand-shake! Leave ole Gabe alone; that boy's getting him some experience." Murray, at nearly eighty, had a gleam in the eye and a bass-clef laugh to remember. "Gabe is my man," he said. "Bring him on by here, sometime soon. I'd like to check him over."

So I did bring him over, and things had gone pretty smoothly. I cut the visit short, declaring victory, and sig-naled Gabe. We stood in the small neck of a hallway in front of the door, and in the midst of the general good-byes Gabe sensed a magic chance for embarrassing his nervous father.

"So, Dad, how did I do?" he said. I shot him a look, and he turned his head on its side, now enacting his question in silence, keeping it in the air.

"You did okay," I said, "Now, let's say good-bye, Gabe. It's time."

But then the Murrays raised Gabe's question with their expressions. So with blood rushing to my head, I had to explain that I'd told Gabe he had to mind his manners and that meant he had to please-and-thank-you just the way he did at his grandparents' place down home. The clatter at the doorway triggered Mister Murray's hardness of hearing, so I had to repeat our once secret warning yet again, with the novelist now leaning forward with an uncharacteristic scowl. When he heard what I was saying, his face relaxed as he leaned back and had to laugh. "His grandparents' place, huh? Well, Gabe, if that's the way you're gonna act, then come on here and give your old granddaddy a hug." Gabe, who at times is simply the most wonderful child in this world, rushed forward with his arms wide, and grabbed Mister Murray around the neck and hugged and hugged. There were more hugs and some sugar kisses for Michele and for Mrs. Murray, too.

And do you know the tears sprang into my old evil eyes—they always do in scenes where father love is so palpable. I left the apartment in a delightful emotional summer storm. When we were alone, I hugged Gabe myself once more for good measure.

"Okay now, Dad, don't forget. You promised me ice cream." That brought me back to earth. We walked outside, and on the street in front of Lenox Terrace the rain-coming heavy winds moved the broken summer leaves in swirls like miniature tornadoes. As we left, Gabe's face lit up. His whole body seemed to say the words with a joy that was absolutely playable on the drums: Yesssss! Ice cream!

That scenario reminded me again of Murray's ideas of lineage and its crisscrossing lines of resonance and bridges of responsibility. For it was Murray who was so unimpressed by Alex Haley and the media's embrace of his family history called *Roots* that he had declared the quest for original deep Southern and then Gambian ancestors not just a fruitless hoax but even a gesture in support of white racism.

At that time he said: "Man, that's what we've been at war against all this damn time: this phony sense of entitlement based on family bloodlines. That's what's kept these white folks so confused and so arrogant. And I mean confused and arrogant for decades, man, centuries! Ain't it just like us to jump up and declare ourselves in support of that mess!"

And then: "The real point is that Alex Haley's actual father as writer—the one who actually matters when it comes to his being a writer, who is basically a slick-style journalist—is nobody but Hugh Hefner any old goddamn way! Hell, don't let 'em fool you, Bob. This Haley ain't no African, man! He ain't nobody but that *Playboy* magazine editor's own brownskin boy!" (He referred to Haley's having written on occasion for *Playboy* magazine.)

All of which invoked a point sounding throughout the Murray canon: the artist is born somewhere of course, linked by birth to particular parents and thus to idiosyncratic styles of living, ways of talking, and values. He or she had better open those doors and explore the home territory (seedbed for what Murray has termed the "idiomatic particulars") if art and artist are to be grounded and steadied for imaginative flight.

And yet—witness Auden and Ellison and Borges—the artist who is bold enough to obey the "vernacular imperatives" of confronting parents and homeplaces and their hard-bought truths must also stake a claim to a set of artistic guides and models; must take the next step of choosing fathers and mothers as artistic guides. Here's the only way the Rabbit gets free of the Tar Baby of yore: by learning, from whoever has the knowledge, the values and techniques of his or her art so thoroughly that freedom is won at last. At least it grants the freedom to find the language to tell how goddamn unfree you feel most of the goddamn time, as Mister Murray might say.

"Your nose is snotty, your head is knotty," my boyhood friend's father used to say to me, "and if you don't know what you doing, Youngboy, ask somegoddamn-body!"

This right to choose ancestors (to ask somegoddamn-body), is of course a right larger than race, and means that Murray is related to Thomas Mann and Ernest Hemingway, to William Faulkner and Andre Malraux, to Ralph Ellison and Suzanne K. Langer, to Kenneth Burke and Constance Rourke. And like a jazz musician—for Murray's sensibilities are also shaped by Duke Ellington's (and Count Basie's and Earl Hines's) characteristic modes of piano vamping and comping and pulling the dirty as well as the sweet notes out of their band player's horns —Murray is then able to take the lessons of those who went before him and then to do that hardest thing of all (which again evokes the powerful example of the jazz musician, that prototype of the committed artist in our time): to find a sound of his own; with it, to tell a story.

And so of course it was not lost on me on that Lenox Terrace afternoon that Murray, in choosing my son to be his grandson, was also making me proud by choosing me, too. Because of which, and because of the imperishable example of my own father (and a briar patch of idiomatic particulars, kicking my idiomatically particular behind), again I thought: Oh, God, somehow I've just got to do better.

Which meant, too, that I was thrown back again to that hot, windless January afternoon in 1969 when I sat in the church at the Halfway Tree, Kingston, Jamaica. Back to some of it, and then back to all, in a silent electric-storm rush of tingling light and then the thunder. Back to seeing that on top of the box that held my father's body was a picture-framelike oval glass opening, just large enough to show his face. He was very neatly shaven, white-and-gray-haired, white-goateed, fifty-eight years old, old for his years. With his eyes gently shut, he looked not so like a man who was asleep as one who was pretending to sleep, playing a part. And somewhere inside me, though I knew he was dead, I imagined his shaking me awake like he did me when I was a boy, assuring me that he was still okay, that it was nothing but a strange sort of initiatory joke, or a hideous, fevered dream, like those I used to have of monster men dwelling in the basement of our home.

For his funeral he wore his best suit, a new item bought, as I recall, for our vacation, cut in what was known as a "Nehru" style—high at the clerical collar and lean of line, like its wearer. My uncles and cousins joined me in carrying him to the newly cleared space in the hilly burial yard just behind the old church building at Half-way Tree.

"Yes, it's a lovely little church and a lovely burial place," said my Jamaican Auntie Nez. She spoke to a group of cousins gathered later that evening at my cousin's place, where the smell of rum hung heavy in the air.

"The goats scampering 'round the gravestones gives it a rustic air, mon," she said. "Very peaceful. But don't go there alone, y'know," she added, turning to address me with special confidentiality. "There are robbers who work that yard from behind the trees and stones and thing. Once I visited there and one o' them did just burst out upon me and snatch my bracelet right from off my arm!" She looked hard at me, as if the loss of the bracelet were still the day's major emergency.

Two years after this saddest of days, when they lowered my father into the ground, my teenage Jamaican cousin Gayle wrote to me at college in California to say that she and other cousins had visited the gravesite and were keeping it neat and clear of leaves and rubbish. It bothered her, though, that there was no marker of any kind at the place. If no one came to check the grave, maybe someone else would be put there, too, she said. Or maybe the weeds would take over the spot and make it impassable and unvisitable. Poor Uncle George would be so unhappy in a bush of thorns, overrun by wild goats. Yes, and thieves, I thought, and their wretched gravesite-visiting victims. I hadn't known that my Jamaican relatives' planning for Daddy's interment did not extend as far as erecting a headstone. The spot was marked by a tiny slate with no words engraved on it, a sad blank marker. ("It's not so often," once said wonderful Mary

Gordon, the writer, at the elevator of our building on the Upper West Side in New York, "that we can do anything for the dead.")

Though unarmed with this wisdom, I had something like this in mind when years ago I responded to my cousin's letter by writing to the U.S. government and asking if, as a World War II veteran, Daddy was entitled to a military burial. If so, please place a headstone at his gravesite at Halfway Tree in Kingston. When, after a flurry of letters, it was done, the inscription read:

SERGEANT GEORGE M. O'MEALLY
U.S. ARMY
BELOVED HUSBAND AND FATHER

I rested easier. I hope he did, too. After all, Mary was right. When would I get to perform my next service to my father, dead now all these years?

(Mary had been talking to me about service to the dead because just this year she herself had become so incensed about her own father's place of burial that she had had him dug up and placed with relatives he had really loved and who had loved him back. She'd even found the original funeral director, who answered her questions about the service and about what was likely to be down there now, twenty years after the burial, by saying, somewhat furiously, that if the family had paid a bit more he'd have had a more durable coffin to rest in!

"As it is . . . well, who knows?" he told her. "Anyhow, the real secret to these things is—guess what?—moisture," he said. "Why, I've dug up bodies from thirty-five years gone by and found them looking as fresh as a new daisy, completely unchanged. But after a few weeks those on a moist spot can fare much worse." In the case of Mary's dad and his box of wood, and, alas, his moist place of rest, the diggers could find no trace of a box at all—or any other remains of any kind. So they dug six feet down, carved a deep rectangle of earth as big as a giant sofa, and carefully extracted it from the ground. With full offices and ceremonies of the church, and with all the family gathered, they reburied this great geometric chunk, scattering rose petals in the hole as they lowered the big piece gently down.)

Daddy, I think, would've been pleased with his spot— a shady play in a churchyard, back in the land where he was born—and would have appreciated the grown-up follow-through involved in his son's seeing to it that the grave was not only marked in marble but also inscribed with his identity as a U.S. citizen, a (noncom) officer.

"You lookin' for that soldier?" I was asked when I last visited Halfway Tree two years ago.

"Yes," I answered. "O'Meally. The American soldier."

What can I say to Gabe, and to his brother, Doug, about the grandfather they never saw, the soldier gone so long before they were born?

Dear boys:

Your grandfather was a long, thin man, a man of angles and elegance who had an invincibly relaxed way about him. He was a khaki-brownskin man with glistening hazel eyes that smiled easily. He wore a mustache that tended toward thickness, an even toothbrush of dark brown and then faded brown and gray hair. In his last years he sported a short, sculpted beard that accented his aristocratic bearing. I remember him as barbershop sharp—ever sharp, but at his best just before he and my mother took off for a formal dance, sleek and slick as a jazz musician. In his youth, as pictures show, he tended to be something of a dandy, with cufflinks, stickpin, cane, spats, and hat turned to an *Esquire*-swanky angle. As a middle-aged man, these foppish qualities were muted somewhat. But he was always a very careful dresser, and it meant something to me that the last clean clothes he ever had on were clean. *Clean*: I mean it in the vernacular sense that he was coiffed and talcum-powdered and clipped to a fare-thee-well. Double-clean, mean and clean.

For all his occasional Jamaicanness—the twice-a-year mango or salt fish from the international grocery store he favored; the sometimes syncopated angle on which his cadence would fall on a word, especially when he was annoyed and the syllabic pulses traveled back home to the blue hills and shorelines of the old homeplace; the sense of rum as the classic drink of drinks both for adult "lil taste" ceremonies and for children's medications (he once had me swirl rum in my mouth to end a particularly painful toothache, and then to swallow it to ensure the pain did not return); and the peculiar sense of outrage that U.S. racial prejudice, to which his upbringing had taught him to be superior—it was a stupid American disease applied inexorably to him, too: To the cracker cops of D.C. he was just another nigger—a phrase that seemed preposterously wrong for this most elegant of men, and a "monkey-chaser" to boot. (This latter was also at times the name he was called by his U.S. black brethren in sadly hierarchical Negro Washington of those long-gone days.)

And yet who was more a Yankee than this gentle man

who came of age in the era of swing? Than this U.S. soldier? I remember him in rushes when I hear certain music that he loved. Like Albert Murray, he was an avid Ellingtonian. I'm sure Duke's own classiness and the ambitiousness of his art appealed to Daddy. He especially loved the sound of Ellington's most favored soloist, Johnny Hodges—so lusty with melody and broad in tone, so effortless-seeming in his bluesy swing, so clear and eloquent in the mysteriously local and yet somehow universal language of serious jazz.

The sound of Nat "King" Cole also evokes my father's memory. He had two Cole records, "Just One of Those Things" and "Love Is the Thing"—both of which reveal the singer's honey-toned, heavy-silken lyric gifts. Here again, as with Hodges, the tone is the thing—or as jazz players say, "his sound." ("Aw, man," you'd hear them say about a new player on the scene, "the dude can play okay, man, I guess, but to me he isn't shit, really, because he ain't got no sound.") Well, Nat King Cole had a sound. And Daddy often told the tale (here I guess is where Caribbean immigrant and black Southern migrant to the North shake hands) of King Cole erasing all traces of his home accent; how he unsouthered his enunciation and unblacked his tone until, as my father understood it, he could sing to the world. Daddy had no particular affinity for the raw earthiness of B. B. King, with whose music he had no direct experience, but neither did he care much for strongly flavored vernacular Jamaican music. Harry Belafonte, though significantly unrepresented in Daddy's record collection of about twenty-five lps, was as close as Daddy came to nostalgia for the old country's music. He preferred his black-label rum with mixers—with Tom

Collins and a twist of lemon. He loved his blues and bal-
lads to be deeply dished but trimmed with Ellington's
big-city subtlety and stylish mix of moods. Not just local
music but music that, without even the tiniest shred or
scar of compromise, can be overheard and enjoyed by the
world.

Dad played a bit of piano himself. Gently lilting and
lyrical, with a few black-key tricks in the place of real
technique, he picked out tunes by ear. One day after
school he shocked me when I brought a saxophone home
on loan from the orchestra by picking it up cold and testing it out by playing a slow ballad—was it "Stardust"?
—squeezing it out with a Johnny Hodgeslike trace of
unabashed vibrato-rich romance. "Yeah," he told me with
his special wink, "it's not a bad horn." Where had he
learned to play it?

He was a good father in so many ways. He laughed
and joked with me, as if we were old friends. He took
me to the playground and taught me to hit fast pitching
when I was eight years old by throwing to me with his
wide sidearm fastball. Later I would be ready to see his
fadeaway curve. He took me to see the Yankees and
loved seeing Mickey and Yogi and Moose as much as I
did. Mantle, who in those days would lift home runs out
of old Griffiths Stadium at a forty-five- or fifty-degree angle, dream-rocketing them over the tall light fixtures into
the blue.

Dad wasn't just doing his duty; we were baseball buddies from the word go. He even let me stay home from
school to sit in the basement with his fellow workers and
army buddies who also were playing hookey to see the
World Series. My job, at such times of English Leather

and Southern Comfort and, always, Appleton Rum was to sit, watch the game, and basically never say a single word. That way I would get to hear the men respond as if I were not there. Sometimes I even got to hear my father tell a tale in his high, thin, cussing voice—a voice and a vocabulary never otherwise heard in our house—with him acting out all the characters' parts and voices.

When I was in Little League (in Washington we called it the Walter Johnson League), he often attended our practice sessions and rarely missed a game. When Mr. O'Meally was around, the boys did their best not to cuss or to say anything their own parents would not stand for. Boo and Half-Head and Cakes and even Cholly learned to respect "Bobby's father." They knew that this quiet, well-dressed man was there for them, too, that in some sense he was the father we all needed and wanted. Pop cheered for everybody, and when we had an "away" game—which meant we were contending for the regional or citywide title—he let nine or ten of us boys ride in the family car, two or three with the bats and catcher's equipment sitting backward in the open-mouth trunk of the car as we bumped through town signaling and (if we won) cheering as we rode back to the Takoma section of D.C., where I grew up.

In fall, 1965, my senior year, I told him I was quitting baseball and concentrating on other interests—writing, music, "politics" (I was president of Coolidge High's student council), parties, girls. One of my happiest memories is of the afternoon Daddy came to me after dinner and said he really wanted me to go out for the team just this last time before I left home for college.

"It really just pleases the devil out of the old man to

see you play," he told me. What tickles me now is that without missing a beat I told him, "Sure, Daddy. If you want me to play, I'll just play." How did I know to say that? He smiled that smile of his that made his eyes twinkle and say Hey! Now we had yet another secret, another bridge.

That year, every game when I first got up to bat, I'd step out of the box for a moment, scanning the stands. "Hey, Bobby!" he called, waving to me. "Hit that ball, baby!" No other memory of him hits me with as complex a dose of joyous energy as that one does. I'd do my Mickey Mantle stance and do my damnedest to hit one to bring the old man to his feet.

Some memories are not unequivocally joyous. One day in August, at the end of the formal league season, I walked to the field behind the baseball diamond that we kids called the knockout field. It was a cool, grassy place with long old spruce trees waving overhead where four or more kids could choose sides and have a makeshift game. Looking back, it fascinates me that in some ways our knockout rules were much tougher than those of regulation play. One swinging strike, for example, and you were out. Ground balls caught by the infielder(s) meant the hitter was out. Sometimes two players, the pitcher-infielder and the outfielder, had to cover the whole field, which, when everything worked, was beautiful to see. No wonder the guys who starred on the knockout field routinely went on to win city titles: At twelve and thirteen, we not only played all the time, we played on rougher fields and with tougher rules than our coaches could have enforced on us. We loved this game with all its graces and, alas, with all its tests and rites of passage.

Onto this field of rough-cut baseball fools and dream-
ers, the city champs that year again, if memory serves,
Bill-Bill, who was not one of the baseball regulars,
brought a brand-new thirty-something-dollar glove. It
was a pretty thing: a Rawlings pitcher's glove, oversized,
with the deep pocket and the web closely woven and the
fingers long and curved to perfection. As I say, Bill-Bill
was never much of a player—a quiet brown boy with
clean, pressed pants and what looked like a new-for-
school shirt buttoned to his baby face, wide-eyed with
wonder. He couldn't have known that he'd fallen onto a
field both of dreams and of nightmares, fallen into the
hold of a ship of twelve- and 13-year-old musketeer veterans of the knockout park and all its sharp-edged, shad-
owy deeps.

Of course Bill-Bill was not chosen to play; his arrival
on the field was unmarked by a greeting of any kind that
I recall. Of course his glove was sighted by every boy for
a city block.

"Lemme borrow that glove, man," Eric said, running
over, pulling it from Bill-Bill's hand. Bill-Bill's first mistake that day was that he was too polite not to say,
"Sure."

"Hey, lemme hold it, Eric," I said. He threw it to me.
I'd known the feeling of a serious new glove. Mine had
once been this way—too stiff to trust in a game, yet as
exciting to the senses as when Daddy brought home a
new car. I threw it back to Eric and put my glove back
on; it was still strong but soft—a well-oiled and limber
extension of my own hand, my much tested weapon in a
centerfielder's struggle against fly balls, liners, over-
thrown tosses, hits through the infield, or anything else

that came my way. My father had taken me with him to buy it and shocked me by getting the most expensive thing in the store. (Here again we encounter the aristocrat's highborn tastes. When this immigrant boy-man looked in the mirror, what he saw was a prince who in a minute or two would take over as the king of someplace big.) As a surprise he had my initials engraved in the leather, concealed just behind the wrist strap. Just like my dad to opt for the elegance beyond elegance implied by a glove monographed R.G.O. As part of my professional name, I always keep that G in there. It stands for George and for a voice that's in my head. It stands for a set of standards I try to keep in mind when I'm with my own two sons.

"Lemme hold that mitt, Eric," said Bucky, Eric's brother. "You don't know what to do wit' no good glove anydamnway," he said. "Let a man have a look, boy, *sheet*!" "Hey, man, lemme . . ." "Hey, Jack, looka here man, I mean, lemme see that shit, man." The glove was passed around and thrown around, pounded in the grass and in the soft infield dirt under a rolling cloud of steamy dust.

As Bill-Bill's glove was making the rounds, the knockout game went on. Eric hit one a mile over everybody's head out into the practice tennis court, an automatic homer. The game was ragged, with players coming and going. (Bill-Bill never played.) Even Cholly, our regular pitcher, suddenly showed up for a while—dressed mysteriously in expensive casual clothes from a store downtown where all the blockboys shopped—and then, just as suddenly, took off. He was a moody kid, a tough little nut who pumped fastballs and roundhouse curves past young batters all over Washington. I knew. I'd watched every pitch for four years from center field.

Anyhow, with night coming down, the game was over, and I made my way through the eight or ten blocks back home. Ready for dinner, I rounded the corner and flew up the steps and into my house. I was through the hall and about to bound up the steps when I noticed that we had visitors.

"Bobby." It was Daddy's most serious voice, calling me in. Uh-oh, I thought. Now I've done it. He's got me this time. And I did it, too, no question about it. But what exactly had I done? I stood at the wide door to the living room, looking in.

I noticed a boy my age standing behind a hulking man. The way the boy was breathing showed that he had been crying.

"Bill-Bill?!" I said. "What's up, man? . . . Daddy, what's happening?"

Then, suddenly I remembered it all. Aw shit, I was guilty. Cholly had put Bill-Bill's glove inside his shirt and disappeared behind a tree at the back of the knockout field. Then he had disappeared with the glove. I had seen the whole thing, but, according to our teammate code, I had said nothing. Bill-Bill was a chump to show off his glove anyhow. He should never have let anyone touch it, not at least without insisting that he get to play. He'd been caught in a chain web of rules and rituals he did not know about, and his ignorance had cost him his glove. Tough shit for him, I thought. What was he doing at my house?

"Mr. Williams here says his boy saw you take his

glove," said Daddy, with his eyes calm but searching mine.

"What!?" I said. " 'What' was a term of surprise and anger that children did not use with adults in those days, so I turned as if addressing Bill-Bill.

"Now, you know me," my father went on. "I want the truth and I want it right now. I told them you are not a thief, that there must be some mistake. But Bill Jr. here remembers seeing you with the glove last."

"Yes, sir." The "sir" came out unexpectedly, always at times like these.

"Do you have Bill-Bill's glove?"

"No, sir, I don't."

Bill-Bill breathed deeply. His shoulders shook. "He's lying," he said.

I turned quickly to face him, but kept quiet. "I should knock your babyfied ass down just for saying that shit," I said to myself. "Glove or no goddamn glove." I glared at my shivering accuser.

"Are you sure?" said Daddy to me.

"Yes, I'm sure. Daddy, I promise."

"Okay, Bill, that's it," said Daddy to Bill-Bill's dad. "I'm sorry about all this, but Bobby doesn't have the glove. If I hear anything, I'll let you know. I know all these boys. I'll see what I can do."

Now the fathers' codes clicked in above our heads. Mr. Williams obviously regarded me as one of the hoodlums of the park who had excluded his son from baseball fun and now had conspired to take his new glove. It outraged him that his son was in this position, and he looked at me like he was just dying to get his hands on me, to slap me to the floor. But he could not disrespect my dad's house by saying anything more to me, or anything at all questioning my father's word or authority.

"I don't know, George," was all he could get out. When he left, the door—with its broken spring—seemed to slam with the rage of both the Bill-Bills, senior and junior.

"Whew," I thought. "I'm glad that's over."

"Wait a minute, son," said Dad. "Now, I held my tongue until they left, but now I have to know."

"Really, Dad. I didn't take it. Why would I? I have a glove. I'm not a robber, Daddy, come on, you know that!"

"Yes, I know."

"So?"

He held my hand gently, in an attitude of urgency and appeal.

"Do you know who does have the glove?"

"Of course," I said. "But come on, Dad, Bill-Bill is a dope, with his big old head. He doesn't even need that glove. And he shouldn' been showing off with it anyway. He shoulda been home learning how to use it. It wasn't even oiled right! Who took it?! Daddy, come on, you know I can't tell that."

Well, I *could* tell, as it turned out, and I did. Under the pressure of my father's softly turned words about "neighborhood" and "the truth" and "growing up" and "winning off the field," I collapsed and said the dreaded name:

"Cholly has it."

"Okay," said Dad. "I'm not surprised. Geez," he said, "I thought that boy and I had an understanding."

"Don't do anything," I said. Never mind civic duty and

doing right and all that, Cholly made my blood stop. There was something unearthly about his concentration as a pitcher. He stared at the target and split it in half with his fastball or sailed in with a dipping curve at two or three speeds. Short and cocky, at thirteen Cholly seemed as tricky and wise as the world and weary of the varieties of bullshit (like school and church and plans for the future) that dummies like me took seriously. The other part was that Cholly carried a five-inch knife, and struck me as quite willing to use it on the likes of me, who, for all my playground bravura, obviously came from a world other than the one he knew most intimately.

Daddy left me at home to eat a dinner of which I have no memory whatsoever, and to go through my other evening routines. I do remember washing those dishes as if my life depended on it. Just before bedtime, Dad was home again, the slamming front door the announcer of his return.

Dear Doug and Gabe:

This is the kind of man he was: When to my mind the simplest thing in the world would have been just to let Bill-Bill and history of the glove and its travels with Cholly just float away like yesterday's dust, my dad took off as if he were the high sheriff of the neighborhood, the true standard bearer. More precisely, he was acting as if he were not only my father but Cholly's, too, somehow, and even Bill-Bill's. Here was fatherlove in fifth gear, fatherlove that would not quit.

He drove the black '61 Chevy the six or so blocks over to Tewksbury Place, that sunfaded street of dwarfed trees that we kids called stink-fruit trees, with their droppings that smeared the pavement during August of every year.

I heard what happened next from my ace boon coon Eric, who saw it all from the sidewalk outside Cholly's house.

"You want to see Junior!?" Mrs. Thomas drew back as her outraged questioning voice shot through the screen door. "And who might you be? You not one the law, are you?"

"No, Mrs. Thomas. I'm George O'Meally. My son and Cholly play ball together at Takoma. He knows me. I'd like a word with him, please. It's important."

Behind Mrs. Thomas was a long, fuzzy staircase to the second floor. Cholly peeped downstairs and then disappeared again.

"He's not here right now," she said. "Can I give him a message, Mr. McNeal?"

"I saw him upstairs, Mrs. Thomas." He spoke past her, up the steps. *"Cholly, come down here. I'm not going to hurt you."*

"Now, you wait just a damn minute, Mr. McNeal," said Cholly's mother. "Don't be shouting into my house and going on. I said Junior ain't home." Her head turned and snapped back and forth now, like a rooster's. She was a very pretty, deep brown woman in a black hairnet who looked like she'd been disturbed from her nap. She was waking up quickly, though, and her patience was fading.

"I'm going to have to ask you to excuse yourself now," she continued. "This has gone too far already, really."

"Madam," said my dad, quietly taking her to Hollywood, "I'm afraid that Cholly has taken a baseball glove belonging to another boy. If he does not return it to me right now, there could be real trouble."

"My Junior did not take any damn body's glove," she announced. "And another thing: You got one helluva nerve marching up to my door in the first place. Who are you?!"

There were more words.

With Mrs. Thomas blowing hard about "her child" and who it was that was "mighty bold," stepping up onto "her porch" and on and on, suddenly a hand threw a stiff blond glove down the steps. Near Mrs. Thomas's feet, it hit the lower landing with a dead thud.

By the time he was home again, Dad had said whatever he said to Cholly, who came downstairs at last, and he had returned the glove to Bill-Bill.

Bill-Bill and I never spoke of this matter again. And from that day on, Mr. Williams always kept me in front of him, as if I were a dangerous dog he'd just love to crack with a stick.

The postscript was supplied by Cholly. The season itself being over, I did not see him again until school time, about a month later. Maybe I had spotted him before then and had just ducked away. Then one day my luck ran out.

Dear Doug, dear Gabe: How can I tell this next part? Cholly saw me from across the school blacktop and changed direction, military-style, to confront me directly. His BanLon shirt (the rage of those days) flashed a pretty orange in the afterschool twilight. I stood completely still. My heart knocked in my chest like a hammer. It's not that I was a chicken. I wasn't. I'd had my share of fights, and I even confess that sometimes I relished the release of energy and anger that went with boxing and wrestling to the finish. But this was not just another fight. I had broken the playground code, and here came hard-throwing Cholly, Cholly with the knife.

He came close up to my face and just stared at me. He was my size but chunkier in build. He was also a year older and ten years more experienced. Then, too, he seemed permanently mad at everybody, which gave an initial advantage in any fight. I had to work myself up and woof and push and carry on, but not Cholly. He was one of Jack London's don't-mind-dying killers, ready to leap through the air and tear your throat out before you had a chance even to paw the ground or snort, much less say anything. I'd seen him on the playground, suddenly punching out someone who had no chance to see the violence coming. Cholly liked to end a fight quick, before his opponent could react. And he always had that long knife. He even carried in the back pocket of his flannel baseball pants, in case of trouble on the field or, especially when we played away from home, after a game was over.

Without thinking, I did what I always did when confronted by "blockboys" like this: I smiled to beat the band. I smiled and smiled. Behind the smile, I watched him, and got ready.

"Hey, Cholly," I said. I pretended to have no sense of the present danger. I was set to be sociable, maybe exchange a few remarks about baseball and stuff like that.

But Cholly was not into denial.

"Hey, *hell*," he shot back. "Looka here, muthafucker . . ." I was ready to pull back from a punch. I knew something about boxing and was ready to dance awhile with Cholly if I had to. But God, no one was around to break us up. I looked at Cholly's fierce eyes and smiled some more. He did not swing at me but just balled up his hands in an unmistakable fury. I got ready to fake with my left fist and then hammer him with my right. I got my hands set and watched his head. If he made any move in the direction of his back pocket, where he kept his knife, I would belt him hard and run. Meanwhile, I just smiled.

"I should kill your lame ass," he said. "And I want you to know that I would do it, too. The only reason I won't is because of your father."

"Did he say he would call the cops? If he did, I'm sorry, man. I told him to leave you alone."

"Naw, dummy," said Cholly. "We shook hands, see? I promised him it was over. Finished." He made a quick gesture of wiping his palms together as if brushing something away. "So it's finished." He turned to go, his gabardine pants snapping as he walked away in a disgusted swagger. He did not look back.

And I was left there, dumb and dirty, stupid with my smile, glad Cholly was gone. Now I was like Bill-Bill, the inexperienced one in need of a witness, the dumbbell. Now I was Cholly, too, the criminal in search of mercy from the court, and getting it, somewhat, being released. Mysteriously, my father had orchestrated the whole thing, had kept the chaos at bay. Somehow in this scene he was father to all three of us, and enforced a code of behavior that kept us, at least for the space of this scene, relatively safe and at peace with one another. I ran home to think things over. It had been quite an encounter, not one I would ever forget.

Dear Doug and Gabe:

Did I tell you that my baseball nickname until I left D.C. to go to college was "Smiley"? Even Daddy sometimes yelled out to me with my handle: "Okay, Smiley, watch out for that curve ball. Hit one for the old man!"

My father died when I was nineteen, while the family

was on vacation. He was buried two days after my twentieth birthday. The event blinded me, and left me more lonesome than I thought the world could be. Could it be that that event, that miserable vacation-time planting, marked the real end of my childhood, the last of poor Smiley? The birth of a confused, hopeful player with words in search of a sound of his own?

I never wanted another father, that's for sure. My own real father was full of humor and fun and elegance and direct-drive courage. He loved me and he let me know it. He protected me and he expected me to be a man worthy of being somebody's husband someday, and somebody's father. He trusted me. He played with me and taught me how to play. And yet because I was so young when I lost him, I have long felt a kind of nervous reverence for older men of talent like wonderful Mister Murray. In the presence of such men, I've long felt a certain watchfulness and care associated, perhaps, with my persistent dream that this time I'll be more careful than ever and even a heart attack can't kill my daddy dead enough for him to be really dead. I'm also aware of my efforts as a writer still in training, of my filial debt to the likes of Ellison, Murray, as well as to Faulkner, Twain, and others whom I admire and whose tradition I want to be part of.

The minister in our church, Riverside Church in New York, is the magnificent Reverend James Forbes. He isn't much older than I am, but his position makes me associate him with authority and the mystique of fathering. Like Murray, Forbes is an intellectual and—when it comes to making and performing sermons—also an artist. As with those I adopt as intellectual and artistic guides and fathers, I listen very hard when Forbes speaks. I listen to the words, I listen beneath the words for the cadences and echoes from other dimensions.

And listening is a key feature of Forbes's sense of the sacred. "Seek that quiet place where you can be the one to whom God speaks a special message," he said one Sunday. "Be part of the Uplift Element. Calm down inside; be quiet enough to hear the voice of God."

And now the confession: That time when during his sermon Reverend Forbes called for total silence, turning that immense space into a country church house, or a side-street storefront in old D.C., I did listen. I listened with all my soul. I listened until I heard the chandelier lightbulbs hum a low, steady note. I heard the old stained windows faintly crack and creak with the changes of temperature. And I then heard a familiar voice—one that I was born knowing and hearing and which I also listen for and, in the Murray sense, choose. A voice from the getting place, it was choosing me, too.

"Bobby," the voice said. "Watch out for that curve ball, son. Go on and hit one for me."

Robin D. G. Kelley

Countering the Conspiracy to Ignore Black Girls

Robin D. G. Kelley is a professor of history and Afro-American studies at New York University. He is the author of Race Rebels: Culture, Politics, and the Black Working Class *and* Hammer and Hoe: Alabama Communists During the Great Depression.

"Okay. Pretend I'm Kimberly and you're Tommy and, oh, you have to be Billy and Rocky, too. Anyway, pretend I'm the waitress in a restaurant and you see me for the first time and ask for the menu and then look up and then say, 'Kimberly, is that you?' Okay? And then you say, 'Would you like to come to my pool party? All the Rangers will be there, and we'll have cake and ice cream.' And then Trini will get really mad because you didn't invite her and she'll be jealous, okay?''

This is how my five-year-old daughter, Elleza, imagines the lifestyles of *The Mighty Morphin Power Rangers*, a horrible, campy, excessively violent television show that has kids mesmerized and parents going broke on Power Rangers toys, clothes, and coloring books. We forbid her to watch the show and refuse to take her to see *Power Rangers—The Movie*, although she does own a couple of Power Rangers dolls and accessories. The Power Ranger craze is simply unavoidable; virtually every kid in the country has a general idea who these Morphin teens are and what color outfits each one wears.* However, Elleza has no detailed knowledge of the Power Rangers, besides the basic fact that this multicultural team of super adolescents fight "evil," derive their power from dinosaurs, and are experts in karate.

Because the Power Rangers are largely a mystery to her, she has to invent their world, their crises, their adventures. Although she is able to create fresh, highly imaginative tales about these dynamic teens dressed in colorful body suits, all of her narratives ultimately lead in the same direction: romance. Usually Billy, Tommy, Jason, or Rocky get in trouble, Kimberly comes to the rescue, and they get married. Occasionally Kimberly is in a bind and one of the boys saves her, but the outcome is usually the same—first love, then marriage, then Kimberly pushing a baby carriage. Romance is the dominant theme, yet in her mind the Power Rangers are not always teens; sometimes they're infants, other times they're toddlers or little kids who magically turn into adults with a snap of a finger. Those who are not romantically involved are usually siblings.

Of course, we try to do the P.C. thing. My wife, Diedra, and I encourage those narratives in which Kimberly rescues the boys rather than vice versa, and we constantly challenge her understanding of heterosexual relationships, which she derives from daily observation, day care, fairy tales, Walt Disney, and perhaps a bit of instinct. We

---

* For the uninitiated, I should point out that in the early version of Power Rangers, Zack, the only black member, wore a black suit and Trini, the only other minority, wore yellow. Yes, you guessed it: she is Asian American.

believe these are very serious issues, and we do the best we can to raise her with a healthy gender and sexual identity, to help her understand and challenge the sexist world she will inherit.

And yet I must confess that, for me at least, Elleza's style of play is far more enjoyable than being kicked in the face by an out-of-control "roundhouse" or karate-chopped in the stomach. Elleza is smart, strong, and out-spoken when she's not feeling shy, but she is also strongly female-identified and takes pleasure in her girl-hood. Yes, I know "girlhood" and "femininity" are social constructions, and we are always reminding her that boys are not necessarily stronger, faster, more heroic, better leaders, or that they should be barred from wearing dresses, and that girls can have short hair, tattoos, big muscles, positions of power, or wear short skirts without inviting sexual assault. But having witnessed my neph-ews and cousins in action, it is hard for me to accept the notion that aggressive behavior among boys is entirely a product of socialization. Little boys, for example, will hurt themselves repeatedly by jumping off furniture or running into walls. It's as if they cannot comprehend the connection between their pain and their actions. On the other hand, most girls I've witnessed, Elleza included, only have to hurt themselves once in order to figure out that flying off the coffee table head first will result in excruciating pain. Indeed, Elleza was among that elite group of toddlers who came to that conclusion via a priori reasoning rather than experience.

Elleza has been described by friends as the classic girl, mainly because she tends to be nonviolent, cooperative, more verbal than physical, and deeply romantic to the point of bordering on utopianism. She has an astounding grasp of language that allows her to employ complex analogies and similes as well create stunning descriptions. When she was barely four years old, for example, she drew a small crowd at the Guggenheim Museum in SoHo when she started giving alternate names to works by Antoni Tapies, an abstract painter who usually titles his pieces by the materials or colors he uses. Elleza came up with evocative titles such as "Midnight Angel," "Rainy Night," "The Day the Sun Escaped," and "Peace."

Perhaps, as social psychologist Carol Gilligan suggests, this is the nature of girls' play.* But these were also the elements of my own boyhood I enjoyed most. My mother taught me to abhor violence, enjoy reading, and to use my powers of imagination to create a beautiful world rather than reproduce the reality surrounding us. I tried to do this while living on 156th Street between Amsterdam and Broadway in New York City, a neighborhood famous for male posturing and escalating violence. Although I spent a lot of time in the library, I made frequent visits to the local playgrounds and fire hydrants. Besides, my older sister's friends protected me from the baby thugs and saved me from the unmanly label of being a "pussy" ("sissy" simply wasn't in our vocabulary).

Yet, if the truth be told, I was never crazy about hanging out at the playground. Not that I disliked the playground: I still have fond memories of those hot summer days when I thought it couldn't get better than this, days when the music was blasting and everyone was laughing

---

* See Carol Gilligan, *In a Different Voice: Psychological Theory and Women's Development* (Cambridge, Mass.: Harvard University Press, 1982).

and joking on the sun-drenched concrete, stealing some shade on the other side of the handball court, using rocks, ballpoint pens, and matches to pop ten-cent rolls of "caps" (in our day, the phrase "bustin' caps" had a more benign meaning). But except for basketball and (later) tennis, I dreaded playing sports and felt extremely uncomfortable in gatherings of nappy-headed eight-year-old virgins bragging about the length of their "dicks" or which fourth-grader they claimed to have "fucked" in the coat room.

When I moved to Seattle to live with my father, "boy culture" (which some misguided social scientists wrongly label "street culture") was thrust upon me with a vengeance. My dad took it upon himself to turn me into a "man," by any means necessary. He insisted that I, not my sister, help him work on the car, he gave me clinics on "da mentals" of basketball (he took all the "fun" out of it), made me field fly balls, and sent me to a summer camp where boxing was strongly encouraged. My most traumatic memory was in the summer of 1974, when he signed me up to play for the Central Area Youth Association football team. I really didn't want to play football but was too afraid to tell him so. I went through the motions, expecting to get cut, but due to an unfortunate shortage of twelve-year-old players that year, everyone made the team. That the coming months would be spent in utter pain and agony hit me when my father took me to an athletic store to pick out my first jock strap and a protective cup.

To be fair, my father was not wholly responsible for my short-lived football career; I also succumbed to peer pressure from friends and relatives who also regarded organized contact sports as a male rite of passage. However, he did establish a climate at home in which becoming a man (i.e., conforming to established gender norms) and learning to respect authority was the raison d'etre for growing up. There was no give and take or open discussion about what we wanted to do or how we wanted to live our lives. He told us what to do and we did it, period. And like his father, he believed in discipline and followed the adage that to spare the rod (or the belt, the Hot Wheels track, the backhand slap) is to spoil the child. Rather than respect authority, we learned to fear it. Indeed, if I had to divide my life into neat historical epochs, I would call my five years in my father's house the "age of terror." To this day, I am afraid to tell him what I really think and dread the thought that he might accidentally discover this book while looking to buy me another one of those "inspirational" Christian fundmentalist paperbacks on how men should lead their families.

Although I lived with my father only a grand total of eight years,* I'm pretty sure his parenting style has had some impact on my own—what exactly, I'm not sure. Because I am raising a girl, most of his little maxims about what it means to be a man have no direct bearing on my parenting problems. On the other hand, it is entirely possible that his utter paranoia about making me a man, manifested in his extreme misogynist and homophobic views, rendered his version of masculinity less than stable, if not downright comical. In other words, maybe his obsession with me becoming a man (i.e., not gay, not weak, not "pussy-whipped") exposed deep insecurities about his

* My mother and father split up when I was three years old. My sister and I ended up living with him and his second wife from 1971 to 1976, after which time we moved back with my mother.

own masculinity and therefore revealed just how precarious "manhood" really is. A simpler, though more likely explanation is that my father, through his own example,
taught me how not to raise a child. Instead of teaching us
to respect authority, for example, his punishments merely
demonstrated to me the futility of violence as a method of
disciplining children. And the hierarchical manner in
which he ran the household reinforced in my mind the lim-
itations of patriarchy as a model for family life. I really do
believe that my commitment to family based on shared
authority, mutuality, and collective decision-making is
largely an outgrowth of having lived—briefly—in a household where we were expected to follow orders and keep
silent unless spoken to. I don't want my daughter to grow
up like I did, feeling helpless and powerless, afraid to say
what she thinks or fight for what she believes in. I don't
want her to grow up in a family where men are the leaders, women and the children the followers, and all trans-
gressors deviants who must be punished. Thus, long
before I cracked open a book on the sociology of the family or on the case against patriarchy, I had concluded that
my father's understanding of fatherhood was extremely
dysfunctional.

Yet, within the current political discourse in African-
American communities, which places a premium on saving black boys and puts the responsibility for doing so
squarely on the shoulders of black men, my father should
probably be regarded as a hero. According to certain popular schools of thought, the delicate balance of corporal
punishment, steady work, family responsibilities, and
father-son interaction on the playing field was the key

to my success, not the "feminine" values my mother instilled into me when I lived with her.

I find this line of reasoning not only questionable but potentially damaging and shortsighted. It not only proposes a limited vision of masculinity, but more important, it signals that the only progressive, useful role black fathers ought to play is raising black boys. We see this discourse clear as day in films like John Singleton's *Boyz N the Hood* and in books such as Baba Zak A. Kondo's *For Homeboys Only: Arming and Strengthening Young Brothers for Black Manhood* and Jawanza Kunjufu's three-volume *Countering the Conspiracy to Destroy Black Boys*.* We see it in the mushrooming of black male academies in inner-city communities, where the curriculum places a heavy emphasis on promoting male role models in the classroom as well as in their reading assignments, preparing boys for "leadership" roles, and building students' self-esteem and sense of masculinity through discipline and responsibility.†

* Baba Zak A. Kondo, *For Homeboys Only: Arming and Strengthening Young Brothers for Black Manhood* (Washington, D.C.: Nubia Press, 1991); Jawanza Kunjufu, *Countering the Consipiracy to Destroy Black Boys* (Chicago: African American Images, 1985–86).

† Clearly, the purpose of these institutions is not to eliminate or reduce misogyny among young black males, for if that was the goal one might expect to find a curriculum that emphasizes women's history, female role models, and issues of gender and sexism. Ironically, one of the most vicious of these attacks on black women generally and feminism in particular was written by a woman: Shahrazad Ali. Titled *The Blackman's Guide to Understanding the Blackwoman* (1990), this highly controversial and vastly popular book caricatured black women as selfish, power-hungry, aggressive, manipulating, and even dirty. She argued that true liberation required that black women return to their traditional African roles as child-care givers and supporters of black men.

Some of the same Afrocentric critics who support black male academies and insist that saving our sons and reestablishing black manhood is the key to liberation are also nudging women into more traditional roles or ignoring them altogether. Thus, while criticizing the media for what they believe are unduly negative images of black women, many contemporary black nationalists have invested more of their energy into reinstituting the traditional family and chastising black women for failing to support black men. Besides being anti-feminist, they tend to place the blame for the behavior of young black males squarely on the shoulders of single mothers, whom they characterize as irresponsible and incapable of disciplining their sons.

By implication, this limited focus on men raising boys not only renders my daughter invisible but makes me an inauthentic black father. There are far, far fewer guides on how black fathers ought to raise their daughters or popular texts on nurturing healthy, strong black girls. Likewise, books specifically for black mothers raising sons are also few and far between. And in my personal case, I'm worse than an inauthentic black father. I'm a traitor to my race and my gender. Why? Because I'm not raising a son, and I have no intention or desire to become a surrogate father to wayward boyz in the 'hood. Not that I'm suggesting that this sort of work isn't important. On the contrary, respect is due to the brothers out there trying to deal with these kids—boys who live their lives as if on a suicide mission.

Even if I had the desire and drive to take up the manly challenge of black fatherhood in the age of black male endangerment, I don't have a whole lot of confidence in my ability to bring a boy up in the manner to which our defenders of manhood are accustomed. I'm not good with my hands, I don't like baseball, fighting, or toy guns, and my wife can vouch for the fact that as a patriarch I couldn't rule myself out of a paper bag. Every time I'm asked to lecture at a boys detention center or neighborhood youth organization, the poets seem to identify with me much more than the regular homies. And during every family picnic hosted by my in-laws on Staten Island, I either end up playing with Elleza the whole time or swapping baby stories with Diedra's female cousins. I've never taken a seat inside the men's circle, where beer and sports are the order of the day. In short, to most black folks who subscribe to the notion that the role of black men is to save black boys, I'm probably not a very good male role model. Three decades ago, Senator Daniel Patrick Moynihan would have characterized me as one of those "dysfunctional" black men who lacked a healthy masculine self-image and needed to enlist in the army in order to attain one.

But the question remains: where is the concern for raising our daughters, and what are the issues and challenges fathers have to face? After all, even in today's world black women not only experience both race and gender discrimination but are potential victims of sexual harassment, rape, battery, incest, etc.—acts often committed by loved ones. Most African-American working women— not unlike other women—are still expected to put in double days, balancing their time between a full-time job, domestic work, and childcare. How should fathers help prepare their daughters for a world where black women are generally paid less than white men and white women, and in some circumstances less than black men, for the same job? How do we explain the underrepresentation of women in positions of authority, or help our daughters navigate a popular culture in which women are often portrayed as passive and weak or as sex objects for male gratification?

These are extremely critical issues whose political import ought to match that of, say, the rising black male incarceration rate in the U.S. Fathers (and mothers) simply cannot afford to ignore the complex problems confronting their offspring who are young, black, and female. Black girls, much more than boys, for example, constantly have to maintain their self-esteem and sense of beauty in the face of a racialist aesthetic that values white skin and straight hair. While this fact is certainly no revelation to African-Americans, we nonetheless unwittingly pass value-laden signals to our children about skin and hair. Besides the media, the point is sometimes made explicit by the way classmates decide who is ugly and who is beautiful, or family members making reference to "good hair" or to the "pretty babies" interracial couples supposedly produce. More often than not, the message is more subtle: a mother complaining about how difficult it is to do her daughter's hair, a father who is always admiring light-skinned women. Indeed, before Elleza turned three years old, she went through a brief phase when she wanted to be a little white girl. The phase passed quickly (at least for the time being), partly because we had always told her she was beautiful, partly because we never tried to compare her with anyone else. At the same time, we would not allow her to speak of someone else's physical appearance in a degrading fashion.

Battling the aesthetic assault on black girls and boosting their self-esteem in a racist world does carry a certain price. To be told incessantly that you're beautiful or cute or gorgeous while boys are told that they're strong, big, and smart reinforces the subordination of women while conveying the message that the only worthwhile possession girls have is their looks. With Elleza we try to teach her to love herself (including her body) while simultaneously playing down her appearance in order to emphasize her strength and intellect.

As most parents know, actions often speak louder than words. If we want to raise girls to break out of traditional gender conventions that reproduce female subordination and male dominance, dads need to be more cognizant of how our behavior and attitudes as men shape our children's understanding of the world. The way we speak to and interact with women and other men, the way decisions are made in the household, the way parenting responsibilities get defined—all of these factors affect our kids' identities. Daughters, for instance, need to see their fathers breaking traditional gender boundaries, but doing so without fanfare. Making a big deal out of transgressing the bounds of gender only reinforces the idea that traditional roles assigned to men and women are part of the "natural" order of things. The standard example is household work, although to make an impact men need to do at least half of all the work and should resist whining or making a big production out of it. Aside from household chores, dads should spend a lot more time with their daughters playing their games on *their* terms. Don't think for a minute that playing with dolls or makeup, hopscotch or jacks, ought to be Mom's domain, or that every

Barbie needs a GI Joe. Those dads who feel uncomfortable playing girls games ought to get over it or get some counseling. By refusing to play "girl's games," men and boys sometimes unwittingly degrade or ridicule girls' activities, which could have a damaging effect on their self-esteem. Besides, these intimate play moments are opportunities to listen to what your daughter has to say, to get a clearer sense of what she thinks about, and for her to know the many faces of Daddy.

Obviously, these brief and underdeveloped insights represent only the tip of an iceberg I'm only just beginning to explore myself. If there is any single lesson here, it is that arming our daughters for the twenty-first century is just as important as arming our sons. And the responsibility for doing so should not fall entirely on the shoulders of mothers (just as the task for turning boys into men should never be relegated to men alone). But what do I give my daughter to help prepare her for the future? What does she need to survive? Of course, there are the obvious things: unconditional love, affection, honesty, a sense of safety and security, independence, responsibility, and a right to her own private world. Hopefully, she'll leave the nest with enormous self-confidence; an unwavering love for herself as a woman and as an African-American; and a critical appreciation for her cultural heritage—again, as a woman, an African-descended person, and as a product of the modern world. I hope she grows up with a healthy and positive attitude toward sexuality as well as an analysis of society that will enable her to embrace and critically engage feminism(s). She needs to recognize that the sex-based limits placed in front of her are not natural but discriminatory barriers designed to maintain male dominance. She also must understand that these barriers are penetrable through struggle, and that a just society cannot exist until they are removed entirely. Finally, she should learn that valuing herself does not mean devaluing others, and that equality does not mean sameness.

Ironically, if Elleza ends up with a little brother I would probably arm him with the same principles. I will love him the same way I love his sister. I will flood him with affection, try to instill the same kinds of values, and place a great deal of emphasis on cooperation and non-violence. He will learn to love his unique blackness, his cultural heritage with all of its multicultural roots, without apologetics or chauvinism. Better yet, through his big sister as well as his mother, he will learn to admire and take leadership from women, and vigilantly reject the idea that men are "superior" or that male dominance is the natural order of things. If we're successful, he too will grow up as a feminist. And like Elleza, I will teach him to love literature (from Toni Morrison to Oscar Ameringer), art (from Akan sculpture to Flemish painting), and music (from Monk to Debussy). If he wants a clinic in basketball or baseball, I'll certainly do everything in my power to encourage him. Given my limited athletic abilities, however, I'll have to send him to a summer program.

But if for some reason Power Rangers are still the rage by the time he hits three or four, I may have to bite the bullet and improve my karate skills.

Delfeayo Marsalis

Negroid Fatherhood

Delfeayo Marsalis is a jazz musician, producer, writer, and performer. He has published articles on music and culture and written liner notes for many jazz albums.

The summer when I was eight years old and my brother Ellis nine was indeed an adventurous one. At some point during those three long months, my parents took us into the country for a rather extended visit with some of our lesser-known relatives. As we drove through Mississippi one scorching hot day, we happened upon a voluptuous and inviting cotton field. My father, in all his wisdom, stopped the car by the roadside, then offered, "Why don't y'all go ahead and pick some of that cotton?" Before we heard my mother's response, up and out of the car we flew. I'll never forget how much the thought of picking cotton excited us both—kind of like we were greeting a newfound yet old friend.

As we ran into the field, Ellis cheerfully commanded, "Let's get back to our roots!" "Okay, on the count of three. One . . . two . . . three!" Well, let me tell *you*. As we snatched up that cotton, we realized simultaneously and separately that picking cotton wasn't the same in real life as the stories you hear about or see on television. The cotton is hidden by leaves, which are protected by thorns—plenty of thorns, both large and small. We walked back to the car dismayed and disgusted, confused and concerned that our father could subject us to such treachery. We had come to understand that along with food in the belly and clothes on the back oftentimes came a foot in the booty, but this was entirely another matter.

With scratched-up and bloody hands, that fifty-foot walk back to the car seemed more like fifty miles. Yes, Shakespeare definitely knew what was up when he said, "Grief makes one hour ten." As we finally made it back to our broken-down and faded Chevrolet, my mother greeted us with kisses and a few crumpled-up tissues, wiping Ellis's hands and comforting my tears. Of course, old Dad let us internalize the situation before stating, in his nonchalant tone, "Whenever you think about bullshitting—remember that."

More than twenty years have passed since the dawning of that particular dusk on the delta, yet the memory remains with me as clearly as drinking this morning's sour milk. Each situation brought upon immediate discomfort, succeeded by an unrelenting aftertaste. I would come to realize that my father, E (Ellis Jr.), raised his six sons in accordance with one very basic principle: He doesn't know everything, but he knows more than me or you—such is the case with any elder.

E is a man of both many words and few words. While he is often prone to share his vast knowledge of politics and life, those examples that most accurately define his philosophical views are always concise and unadorned. E is a believer in a sharp pencil, an old dictionary, and a big stick. In the tradition of great Negro preachers, he is able to present a coherent story, dip into related and unrelated issues, tie up the loose ends, and take you home with a shout chorus. In the course of a discussion, he will inevitably present views that you: (1) have thought of, (2) have not thought of, (3) wanted to think of, (4) didn't want to think of, or (5) wish you had thought of.

In my personal estimation, many Negroes today would benefit immensely from one day of picking cotton from sun to sun. Either that or hanging out with E. Maybe both.

Through the course of this chronicle, I will provide commentary with virtually no reference to my mother, Dolores. That's primarily because D deserves her own chapter or maybe even a complete book. Emotional D and provocative E. To mention one without the other is like shooting one die and expecting snake eyes. Yes, what a perfect couple Mom and Dad make. D and E. E and D. Mild-mannered E and uncompromising D. Funny how parents always wish they could have done it all over again so they could change things (and mess everything up). Traditional yet not conservative. Old D. And E.

Although I look to old E for guidance in every conceivable capacity, he is quite a difficult man to describe. E. Man first, father second, musician third. But don't come to a hasty conclusion about that order. I would venture to say that the most successful aspect of his parenting was not burdening six sons with the personal judgment and character defamation that often accompanies parental supervision. Rather than incessant nagging, E showed by example.

His way was never "What I think you should do is . . ." but "Well, have you ever considered . . ." Ask his opinion and he'll tell you without prejudice, almost to a fault. Believe me, E wore the pants in the house, yet was always supportive of his sons' decisions, whether he agreed with them or not. Though he often worked for long periods of time during certain years, I can't recall a moment in my life when I had reason to question his patriarchal dedication. One need not be physically present in order to have a great impact upon his children, provided his position is firmly established in their minds.

What type of man would teach school from ten to five and play cocktail piano from five-thirty to ten-thirty five days a week, anyway? E. Easy to take that type of dedication for granted when you are on the receiving end. Me, my brothers, (not my mother), the students, the school board, thousands of hotel guests who relaxed and negotiated to the mellifluous sounds of an honest Negro pianist. "Play it again, Sam. That's what he's supposed to do, isn't it? Entertain us. I don't really care what he plays unless I'm trying to woo. Yeah, just like good whiskey. Sometimes he helps me to remember, but usually helps me to forget."

No matter what the predicament, E will be honest and, most important, not very emotional. Hell, I even asked him about matters of the heart recently—well, one particular matter. Funny how few times a man will tell his son, "I love you" or vice versa. Even funnier how awkward the moment is when it does occur, and how both of us are just glad it's all over with and won't happen for another ten years. But it's cool. I appreciate knowing that a man loves me without acknowledgment of the fact. Don't have to worry about a barrage of "I love you's" camouflaging action to the contrary.

My father, like his father, is a very proud man. In his catalogue of stories, the ones pertaining to segregation are not always the most frequented, but among my favorite. E will tell you about riding behind the "colored only" screens with a hint of melancholy, which is quickly over-shadowed by his misanthropic optimism. Specific memories of segregation are not so important. In retrospect, E doesn't view his life as a series of events, but as stages of comprehensive development, while his ears are open to just about any subject matter, race politics is often a re-curring theme.

I guess every son craves knowledge about his father's ascension above adversity and growth into manhood; about his passions, desires, and subsequent compromises; about his mistakes and pains—not so much to avoid them, just to hear about them. A large portion of growing into manhood as a Negro here in the "land of the free" has maintained consistent over the years. The path to Ne-grodom is paved with a continuous defining and redefin-ing of one's personal worth and perceived societal value.

"At one point," E will tell you, "parents were always convincing their children, 'You are as good as anyone else,' or 'You are somebody . . .' statements that were by their very nature admissions of defeat. Then after King Jr. was assassinated, his lifetime of incomparable achieve-ments was reduced to a dream. And you know what dreams are . . . fantasy. There seems to be a great deal of confusion among today's generation. Nobody really says anything. Seems like we're waiting for this era to end or move on to something else."

I thought about what E said, as I often do, examining my own life experiences. What affects my people most often? Drugs? Crime? Poverty? No. Race matters. The others are a result of the latter. How can I avoid them? It might be a waiter, a cab driver, a teacher, a student, a stranger, a friend, a flight attendant, a store clerk, a newscaster, a magazine writer, a police officer, or maybe two different police officers. Stay in the house with no TV or radio, have food and clothes delivered to the gate and leave the money. What about work? Could do phone sales and avoid any race issues. No, I know—move to Europe or Asia (too much apartheid in Africa). Just run away. Wanted to suggest these things to E, but he'd probably whup my ass. Hasn't done that in twenty years. Still wouldn't have the answer.

"What can I do to make a difference or effect a real change, E?" questioned his fourth son. "In the final analysis, you're either part of the solution or you're the problem. If you hate the problem, well, that says a lot about how you feel about yourself."

After spending two extra years in college trying to figure out what to do with my life (and prolonging the inescapable move to the Big Apple), I decided to move back home. Down in New Orleans the folks have a vibration altogether different from anywhere else on the globe. *Everyone* has some soul, whether they realize it or not. When I moved back to the Crescent City many people had opinions about what would be the "proper" residential environment. "Buy the least expensive home in the best neighborhood." "You want to live out in the suburbs away from crime, bruh." "Move somewhere with a great neighborhood watch." A corner house in a predominantly black neighborhood was out of the question for most, but not E. E had the vision to see many things, a few of which I am only now beginning to comprehend.

See, my parents always insisted that our family live in a Negroid community. It seemed quite odd to me that of the first four sons to move out of the house, the youngest would be the only one to follow his path. What can I say, D & E's strict insistence upon maintaining a strong family made an indelible impression upon me. I had no idea what type of dedication and fortitude was required. Still don't . . . not really.

"One thing's for sure," according to E. "Talking about a problem is vastly different from living in the middle of it, adopting a philosophy, and addressing it in hand-to-hand combat. Malcolm X and Martin Luther King, Jr. We're always talking about what needs to happen in the community. First of all, a community is a group of people with common ideas and goals in mind. We have neither. Second, it's customary that individuals leave an environment to accrue knowledge and wealth and then return. We do half of that. As a result, other people benefit from our advancements. Furthermore, once they integrated us, we gave up everything truly indigenous to our culture— excluding music and athletics—so we could chase after those M.A.'s, Ph.D.'s, and B.S.'s. The schools are set up now so that anyone who doesn't qualify based on another people's criteria has no hope of development on a serious level." The great Negro enigma—the journey to success takes you further from yourself every day.

I remember quite recently E's great struggle with the transition from "Negro" to "African-American." Now, you have to realize that there are few people alive today who are more American than E, regardless of their family history. He is not one to sit around complaining about going back to Africa or colored folk obtaining an independent state somewhere. No sir, not E. He is a family man, a community man, a New Orleans man, a Louisiana man, an American man. That's why his outlook, though terribly cynical at times, is undergirded by a peculiar optimism that only a Negro man living in the South could possibly sustain.

"What do you think, E?" I asked solemnly after describing my latest school debacle.

"Well, that can't be addressed in a sentence or two. See, I actually know some Africans who currently reside in America. So, if *they* are African-Americans, I don't qualify because I have a cursory knowledge of African culture and history at best."

Humph. Yet another reminder of how most people take things for granted in what E terms "our current state of inflamed lethargy."

"But, Dad, they say Negro comes from *necro*, which means dead."

"Man, look. They will say anything. I remember when we went from being colored to Negro. What connotation does colored have?"

Another question . . . no answer.

"People today are more insecure about being descended from slaves than we were in my generation. It sounds more noble to say, we are descended from kings and queens. Now, knowing about those kings and queens is another story. Slavery is not a situation for which the modern-day American should be embarrassed, but an experience which must be embraced and thoroughly examined. That an entire race of people could rise triumphantly in the face of such adversity is not a minor accomplishment. The significance of our ancestors being kings and queens in Africa is only relevant for individuals who have a thorough understanding of the tremendous legacy which has been cultivated right here on American soil." Stories told and untold, songs sung and unsung . . . so exists our history. And a retrospective history always ends in the beginning.

Given the unfortunate yet systematic destruction of the black family structure during slavery, it is remarkable that we enjoy any level of unity as a people. Today's youth face the unenviable task of sustaining the rebellious nature inherent in adolescent tendencies, while preparing themselves for the inevitable responsibilities of adulthood. The former is a gift from nature, while the latter will require guidance from our elder statespeople.

When an elderly person is buried, a library is also entombed.

Slim

"You want to know what's going on in your neighborhood, just find the businesses that deal with the four major commodities and check out who owns them," E decreed. "Where does the money come from? Where does it go? Usually the same place. About the only thing we still own are barbershops. Those brothers can tell you about your neighbors 'cause they've watched them all grow up from babies."

The heart of the Negro community is the church, and one major artery is definitely the barbershop. Like the

church, the barbershop used to serve a utilitarian func-
tion: important meeting place, financial lending institution, forum for sociopolitical debate, educational setting,
and just a place to hang. Back when you had to recite the
Constitution and pass ridiculous testing in order to vote,
men would meet at the barbershop to study. Up at Slim's
barbershop, one of the older mirrors reads, "No loans
without items of value." Of course, you can't miss the
multicolored crayon sign, "Slim cannot lend out no more
money no, no, no. Cause the dirty @#$%&*+@# don't pay
back. Please don't ask Slim." One sign serving notice of
what was; the other, of what is.

Now, Slim is quite a soulful elderly brother who works
six days a week from nine to eight. If you strike up a
heavy conversation, though, he just might very well be
in his high chair counseling you until nine or ten. In his
estimation, "Anybody can make a baby, but it takes a
man to be a father." Just like the renaissance of jazz music
in the 1980s had to bring the music back where it was in
the sixties, we have to get back to where we were socially
in order to move forward. "In the seventies, men stopped
being responsible, the women started working and lost
respect for the men. And with this welfare, plenty of
women will tell you, 'The government is my husband.' "

Slim reminisces about the days when haircuts were fifteen cents and brothers had their own companies. In fact,
several business owners share the opinion that segregation—in spite of its moral delinquency—was not all bad.
"Negroes had to own businesses 'cause we wasn't allowed to go everywhere. Today we're integrated and
there isn't one quality black hotel in this city. No high-
class entertainment either. But don't be fooled. There are

Negroes in this city with some money. They just don't invest it in their people, only in themselves."

Speaking of jobs in all-white hotels, and of an atmosphere that somehow seems foreign to those born after the civil rights movement, the friendly hair stylist maintains an air of sophistication and calm in his voice. "People are confused about what's important. I heard a man who grew up in the country with fourteen brothers and sisters say his father was ignorant. All the children had the same mother. How can an ignorant man provide for fifteen children and a so-called educated man is struggling with two?"

Like most Negro barbers, you can come by and talk to Slim anytime, and he will hear out what you have to say—if it's meaningful. His boys come by frequently to co-sign or dispute his claims, but their opinions about society today are quite congruent. The men from his generation are a proud group. They not only readily welcome change, but are also inspired by any youngster trying to accomplish (or even ask about) anything. "It's y'all turn, now." At Slim's age, he provides a strong reminder of a time when things were incorrect in America but correct at home. Without using the Lord's name in vain or speaking common escapist's rhetoric, Slim states firmly that we must get back to God. "That's the only way we'll get our act back together as a people."

I left Slim's barbershop full of energy and inspiration. Slim is one of many who find rejuvenation and joy among his people. He made me realize that European ideals have taken us away from the elements that are uniquely Negroid and consequently valuable to our sustenance. Slim helped me to understand why I love to live amid the urban turmoil that is so often distorted by the media and popular culture. Plus he gave me a good ass cut and a shave for under $10.

Octobre 26, 1989

Dear Dad,

I arrived in Boston safely. Yeah, the usual thing at the airport. Ticket agent asking me, "Are you flying first-class today?" Of course, I'm too black for this to be a regular occurrence. Anyway, the cab driver greeted with the news of these brothers who have car-jacked some white man and his pregnant wife from the hospital and brought them to the projects (four blocks from where I'm staying at Joya's crib) and killed the woman.

How am I supposed to respect myself and support my people when we resort to this? I don't appreciate slavery either, but is this the solution? I did everything I could not to cuss the cabbie out, but I could see his point. Then he had to start with his "You're not one of them, though" rhetoric. Damned if you are, damned if you're not.

Novembre 5, 1989

Son,

Often we look for answers when there are none on the surface. It's important for the media to portray all Negroes like the unfortunate ones who claimed this woman's life. But they will have to answer to the Creator of those lives they took. Always remember that he who trumpets his shortcomings more than his strengths is forever doomed. Stay strong. E.

January 4, 1990

Dear Dad,

Ain't that some shit? Charles Stuart done killed his
wife and claimed some Negroes did it. Damn. I don't
know whether to feel relieved or disgusted. You know
when a black man kills a white woman there's hell to
pay. The police harassed every brother in Boston that
didn't work for or act like Mr. Charlie. Now they can
only say, "Oops. Sorry, boy, we didn't really mean it."

January 11, 1990

Son,

Apparently Charles Stuart knew our history better
than we do. See Paul Lawrence Dunbar's "The Lynching of Jube Benson" from the late 1800s. E.

Colored Memories

Dad,

Well, the jury's in. Funny, I never quite thought of you
as the militant type. Primarily because militancy is generally associated with violence or activity, not intelligence
or foresight. Nonetheless, I guess I should say that I love
you, that I miss you, that I appreciate the suffering and
sacrificing you did for me. I only wonder, though, if you
really had the right idea—sending me to those schools
around all of them white folks. I know, I know, "Well,
the black folks make it hard on the rest of us because they
act like whitey wants 'um to act—ign'unt."

I don't see where white people have the answers to
everything, even if they own just about everything. Shit,
I sound like you, now . . . "white folks this, white folks
that, black folks this, black folks that." Like all white people sit around with the same philosophy thinking the

same thing, and blacks, too. What I been tryin' to figure out is, where do we fit in?? Martin Luther King thought there was a problem and a solution, promoters of the problem, and seekers of the solution. Negroes have forgotten how great he was because he didn't start every phrase with "black" or "afro." He realized that there are too many different kinds of people for that black and white shit. Humph. I wonder how he felt when he put his head on that pillow every night realizing how hopeless it all was. He was too intelligent not to have realized that. By the time Malcolm X realized it, his own people had him offed. Well, I didn't actually come here to talk about them, anyway. I came to tell you what my most vivid childhood memories are. As many happy moments as I had, those aren't the ones that are the clearest in my mind today.

I remember how adamant you were about me going to Our Lady of Perpetual Help with them, even though I wasn't bussed as part of some deregulation, or whatever it's called. I can see now how tough it must have been on those kids, having to deal with their own questions about life, formulate their own opinions, and make sense out of their parents' ignorance. When you're in second grade, you kind of take adult things for granted. Like, to us, their parents were Mr. Charlie and Miss Betty; to them, our parents were Rufus or Beulah. Do you know how hard it is to respect your father when you see a little kid call him by his first name? Of course you do. I remember that the only Negroes on the faculty were the custodians and the cooks, and that was one clean-ass building with some good-ass food. I couldn't understand why P.S. 26 wouldn't have as clean a building or as good a food, though, seeing as how they had the same type of faculty.

Well, now to my memories. Remember that first Christmas when all the students had to exchange gifts? *You* spent two hours picking out a "respectable" item for me to give to that white kid—that's right—a battery-operated G.I. Joe with accessories. He seemed really surprised when he opened that package, just like I was when I opened mine. A stuffed monkey. I guess his folks spent about five minutes getting that one. 'Course, it took me *ten years* to get it.

What about that time me and Terry called up Lisa in the second grade? He bet me a quarter that I wouldn't ask her for some pussy. Well, when her mother answered the phone, I identified myself and then proceeded to ask old Lisa to give me some of that pussy. Not like I demanded it or anything, I just asked and hung up the phone before I got an answer. She didn't come to school for two weeks after that, and the principal, Sister Lucy, told me I'd be expelled if I ever said anything to her again. Never got my quarter, either.

The next year, there was the kid whose parents sent a letter to the teacher insisting that he be moved out of the seat next to mine. When Mrs. Trapani read that letter in front of the whole class to explain that she must comply to the parents' request, I felt just like what I was—a son of a slave amid the sons of slave owners. Even though I tried to comfort myself with the knowledge that I was the only student to have a desk all to himself for the year, it didn't justify the feeling of rejection and complete isolation I felt. No physical ass whipping could have amounted to this type of psychological torture, 'cept maybe a bullwhip on a Thursday.

You know, they used to make us read *Little Black Sambo*. I don't think it would have been quite so bad if they had left out those damn pictures. Those white kids used to love Sambo, with his big lips and stereotyped ignorance. I didn't realize at the time that they either saw me as Sambo or that they would grow to see me as him. You never did let me associate myself with Sambo, but I wished that you had explained to me that I was Sambo before I found out on my own.

What about Huckleberry Finn and Jim? You know, seventh graders aren't wise enough to know exactly what Mark Twain was trying to say. And I definitely wasn't wise enough to figure out why *I* had to read all of the passages that used the word *niggers*. Ms. Francisco would always kind of giggle when she asked me to read aloud, so the class kind of associated me with that word in an innocent type of way—not like when they heard it at home, I guess. I've pretty much forgotten all of the students' names by now, as I'm sure they've forgotten mine. But I often wonder if they remember me at all. We had some okay times, I guess, as long as we were at school by ourselves. I figure they didn't have many birthday or Christmas parties, anyway. Even if they had, I couldn't dance, so I would have had to stand around looking silly.

I must say, though, that I love you dearly for letting me play little league football for Morgan Park. The brothers used to always break on me—call me a momma's boy because I could never go to a practice without parental guidance, but that was cool. The greatest night of my life was that game we played against Greenlawn when I was twelve years old. Remember that? We showed up with our raggedy jerseys and jeans, while they had brand-new outfits with *Evergreen Appliances* written on the backs with shiny black numbers and everything. "Just like the Americans and the British in the Revolutionary War," you boasted, "let's kick some rump." Seems like their bleachers were filled with the parents, brothers, and sisters of each player, while we only had you, Mr. Burton, and Mrs. Dennison on our side.

I was so proud when our coach didn't show up that night and you told the referee, "No forfeit tonight, bruh, I'm the coach and we've come to play ball!" Remember that? Fourth quarter, we were behind 14–13 and drove down to their goal line in the last minute of play. Then the refs wouldn't let us call a time-out and blew the whistles before we could get a play off. You know, the thought of white people lying or being dishonest had never occurred to me. I guess we're just lucky that the Revolutionary War wasn't refereed by British officials, huh? I remember how much you tried to convince us that we had done good and given our best effort, even made us shake the opponents' hands after the game. You were so quiet the whole way home, though. I could see in your eyes that feeling of dejection and helplessness that I felt after Mrs. Trapani had read that letter to my class.

Well, things got better once I got to high school, though, once all my friends realized that they were white and I wasn't. Thanks to them I was forced to deal with my own people and what truly makes us special. I started to notice all kinds of things when I was around you and your business associates, around Mom and the other mothers. Remember that time Mr. Pennybaker didn't recognize us in that parking lot and he went into a lightweight panic about whether or not we would take his money, or his car, or maybe even some booty? He pretended he was on the wrong parking level and started back towards the stairs.

"Phil, that's your Volkswagen on the end," you said.
"Oh, hi, um, er . . . I didn't, uh, see you standing there. I thought, uh . . ."
"It's cool, Phil. After slavery anything is cool."
"Aw, come on with that slavery shit, man. You always talk about that stuff like I'm responsible for slavery."
"But you are, Phil. The only problem with y'all is that you think we're responsible. We're responsible for something else, though."

Man, I had never checked you out on that vibration so strong before. In that instance I could start to sense a profound militancy. Not all that flag waving, "white man is the devil" crap, but a more refined, contemplative type of militancy. Now that I'm on my own, I see what you were trying to tell me with more brilliance and clarity every day. Like what you said about Mike Tyson, a heavyweight champion of the world—not just of the United States, supposedly champion of the world—gets six years of his life in jail for a very questionable rape. Then all the pictures of Tyson after his trial portray this brutal animal who must be chained and shackled on his way to prison, just as the slaves were. Well, Jeffrey Dahmer killed and ate seventeen people, and I never once saw a picture of him even in handcuffs, let alone shackled.

Guess they only showed Dahmer from the chest up on the news accidentally. Now he seems like the type of person that should be executed or even lynched, but he, unlike Tyson, receives the basic respect that any mass murderer should. Why are mass murderers always white, anyway? I thought you might appreciate that one. Well, I wanted to tell you all of these stories as a prelude to the Rodney King verdict. You were right. Remember what you said in our very last conversation?

"As much as I despise that Rodney King and what he stands for, I could never feel about him as much as I despise people who they are going to acquit for whipping his ass like a slave. 'Cause no matter what I've tried to accomplish and how righteous we've lived, when the gavel falls I'm just another "nigger." I am Mike Tyson and Rodney King, Emmitt Till and Medgar Evers."

Me, too, Daddy. Me, too. Kiss D for me.

Charles T. Ogletree, Jr.

Fatherhood:
If You Buy the Hat
He Will Come

*Charles Ogletree is a professor of law at
Harvard Law School. He is co-author of the
recently published book* Beyond the Rodney
King Story *and a frequent contributor to the*
Harvard Law Review, *among other
publications. He was profiled in Sara Lawrence-
Lightfoot's compelling book* I've Known Rivers
*and has also been featured in such publications
as the* Boston Globe Magazine.

In the commercially successful movie *Field of Dreams*, Kevin Costner plays the role of an Iowa farmer who has what appears to be a crazy idea. Costner has a dream that tells him that if he converts the cornfield in his Iowa farm into a baseball field, it will attract some of the greatest stars ever to play the game of baseball. In a dream Costner is told, "If you build it, they will come." Taking on this challenge, he builds the baseball field, and in fact, it does soon attract the great players of the day. This combination of dreams and symbolism is quite important to me, because it reminds me of an interesting exchange with my father.

Charles James Ogletree, Sr., was a very proud man. He was born in Birmingham, Alabama, and was the second of six children. Although he was able to read and write, and had excellent oral skills, he had little tolerance or patience for formal education. He dropped out of school in the fifth grade.

As a young man, my father decided that the racism and segregation in Birmingham was too much to take, and he headed west, hoping to find better opportunities. After serving in the military for a few years, he landed in Richmond, California, which is north of San Francisco. He ultimately moved from Richmond to Merced, in the San Fernando Valley. That is where he met and married my mother.

My father and I always had a close relationship, and he treated me well. In fact, I would venture to say that as his first child, I received preferential treatment. I don't ever recall him punishing me, although I am sure that on occasion he did. I do recall him punishing my brothers on occasion, and often in very painful ways. While we never had deep conversations, we would always chat about events of the day, including how the Los Angeles Dodgers and San Francisco Giants were doing. He loved baseball and would listen to games on the radio late into the evening. He also was a boxing fan, gathering all of us around the TV on Friday nights to watch the Gillette-sponsored fights on a weekly basis. He was a big and strong man, and was known around the community as "Big Elnido." (There was an African-American town known as Little Elnido.) When he wasn't listening to baseball games or watching boxing, he was very active as a seasonal worker, including hauling hay and working as a truck driver for local contractors in Merced.

My father and mother were divorced when I was still in elementary school. It was difficult for me to accept this. My mother, Willie Mae Ogletree, did an excellent job of raising us as a single parent. Even though my father did not live in the home, he stayed in the same town and would often visit us. He also remembered to give all of us the opportunity to come to his house to collect coins from his dresser drawers, and he also would remember all of our birthdays and see us on appropriate holidays.

He was not reluctant to invite himself over for meals, as often as every other night. My father would also invite us down to the pool hall for dinner, take us out to drive-in restaurants on occasion, and would give us allowances when he had money available.

Despite these very intimate and warm relationships with my siblings and me, there was something lacking in my relationship with my father. I recall that on many important occasions he was not present. My graduation from high school was the first of these. By the time I graduated, I had been elected as the first African-American ever to serve as student body president at Merced High School. I had also received several academic scholarships, and had decided to attend Stanford University. I looked forward with anticipation to my graduation and having parents there to celebrate it with me. As we marched onto the fields to receive our diplomas and other awards, I was struck by the fact that although my father had promised to be there, he did not appear. I was a little shocked, but assumed that maybe he had to work, or some emergency had come up, or that he was ill. In any event, he never gave me any explanation, and it nagged at me for some time.

When I went to Stanford, I found a whole new world. I explored things about life that I had never learned as child, that gave me a sense of increased awareness of world events, and interest in trying to change the world. It was an amazing experience for a young country boy, and transformed my thinking and actions.

My academic career at Stanford was also successful. I was able to graduate in three years, Phi Beta Kappa, and to receive my bachelor's degree with distinction. I also had served as chairman of the Black Student Union and co-president of the student body. I had the occasion to travel to Africa to participate in the Sixth Pan-African Congress and also joined a student delegation on a special trip to Cuba. I also was able to use my fourth year at Stanford to receive my master's degree in political science. As well, I met and later married my wonderful wife, Pamela Barnes Ogletree, who was an undergraduate and equally active in student government. I could not have asked for a better four years.

As I prepared to graduate, I received notice that I had been admitted to Harvard Law School. I was excited to take on this big responsibility of going east and looked forward to a long life with my wife. Both Pam and I were excited about our graduations and anxious to have our families share them with us. We invited a number of our relatives, precisely because we were the first members of our families to go to college and to graduate. Pam's mother and father, brother and sisters, and other relatives came to Palo Alto for the ceremony. My mother, uncle, brothers and sisters, and other friends and relatives came as well. My father had promised to come, and I expected that he would show up. However, to my bewilderment, he did not show up. As much as I enjoyed the pomp and circumstance of graduation, there was something missing. Our graduation was also special in that the black students, outraged at the public comments that professor Daniel Moynihan had made about single-parent families, particularly black families, arranged a major protest during commencement. We planned to walk out the moment Moynihan stood up to be the commencement speaker. We held perhaps the first ever separate graduation ceremony for black students, inviting all of our parents to come a day early so we could praise our mothers for all of their efforts to make it possible for us to be in college. I was surprised to see how many black students had also been raised by single parents.

The next day, at the time of Moynihan's address, we walked out of Frost Pavilion, and were amazed that we were joined by many of our other graduating students, including non-minority students. At the conclusion of Moynihan's speech we returned, participated in the remaining ceremonies, and received our degrees. As we walked out during the protest, I remember assisting the grandmother of one of my friends who also was graduating. I asked her why she was leaving, and she said, "Because I believe in your cause." This same woman had marched with Dr. King in Atlanta decades earlier, and had sacrificed much to make it possible for us to be there. I imagined how important it would have been for my father to see this demonstration of unity and to experience the power of this event. However, he was not there and he was sorely missed.

At Harvard Law School I again was successful. I was able to serve as the national president of the BALSA as one of the editors for the *Harvard Civil Rights-Civil Liberties Law Review*, and to participate in many transforming events, including demonstrations in Washington during the litigation in the *Bakke* case. My wife and I also had our first child during law school, a son whom I named after my father and me, Charles Ogletree III. While at Harvard, I would frequently talk to my father and let him know how things were going. We also had more conversations about the issue of race, and he would occasionally share, with my prodding, some of the instances of racism that he had experienced in Alabama and elsewhere. He also expressed some of his concerns about law enforcement, since he had been arrested on various occasions throughout his life. These talks were a revelatory experience for me, for I was able to understand that some of the problems and concerns I had as a young adult were experiences that my father had, in a much more racially segregated and discriminatory society, decades earlier. We seemed to grow closer as I moved farther away. As my conversations with him increased, I believe he had a better sense of my objectives in life, and I began to understand, partially, some of his difficulties as a young black man in America. While he would talk about racism, he never completely blamed racism for his lack of education, or employment skills, or any other reason for less than a successful life.

Graduating from Harvard Law was, of course, another exciting occasion. Getting a professional degree at one of the most prestigious law schools in the nation was a big event for me and my family. I asked my father whether he was coming, and his excuse seemed more plausible this time. He first stated that it was a long way to come and that it would be difficult for him to travel that distance. Although he did not outright say no, he left very little opportunity for me to believe that he would come. When he did not show up, I was disappointed but not surprised. A pattern had developed: for a variety of reasons he was not going to participate in these public events that in some way shaped my life.

After graduating from Harvard Law School, I went to Washington to take on the job of lifetime, a public de-

fender in the District of Columbia. It was the most exciting and rewarding legal experience I had ever imagined.
I was very successful as a public defender, and very ac-
tively involved in the community.

After several years of practice, my public-defender
peers and I decided that we would like to be admitted to
Bar of the United States Supreme Court. To be admitted,
you must pay a fee and have a member of the Supreme
Court Bar make a motion in support of your application.

In a long shot, I called my parents, told them about
being sworn in before the Supreme Court, and urged
them to come. My mother readily accepted, and my father, consistent with his style, indicated that he thought
it was a great idea and that he would try to make it. To
add a little incentive to this event, I also told him that I
had finally spoken to his brother, Robert Ogletree, who
lived in Buffalo, California, and whom he had not seen
since he had left home in the 1940s. It amazed me that
these two brothers, who had corresponded on a regular
basis over the years, had not seen each other in so long.
Reluctantly, and to my great surprise and pleasure, my
father finally agreed to make reservations to come to
Washington. I could not have been happier.

I looked forward to the swearing-in ceremony with
great anticipation. I would get a chance to have my father
sit in the same courtroom with Thurgood Marshall and
the other presiding Supreme Court justices. For me, Thurgood Marshall was a symbol of both the greatness and
sadness of the African-American experience. Marshall
was about my father's age, and they had experienced the
same kinds of racism and discrimination throughout their
lives. My father had lamented the fact that we live in a

racist society but had no power to affect a change in our society. On the other hand, Marshall used his legal training and skills to transform our society, and argued against all forms of racism and discrimination. It would be an occasion for my father to thank Thurgood Marshall for his great accomplishments over the years, and for Marshall to see that his actions had changed my father's life and created opportunities for me that were not imaginable thirty years earlier. I could not have imagined a greater set of circumstances coming together as we prepared for the ceremony.

The day before the ceremony was scheduled I received a telephone call from my father. The conversation is as clear to me today as it was when he made the call:

> "Junior," he said.
> "Hey, how are you doing?"
> "I'm doing fine, everything is okay."
> "Are you guys all set and packed and ready to go?"
> "Well, I don't think I'm going to be able to make it."

I froze. I could not believe, after all that we had gone through, that my father was not be able to come. We had talked about it for several weeks, I had sent him and my mother tickets, they were packed, and at the very last minute he was canceling. I also could not believe the added incentive of seeing his brother was not enough. However, I was not going to give up that easily. The conversation continued:

> "And, why aren't you coming?"
> "I don't have a hat."
> "What?"

"I don't have a hat, and I can't travel without a hat."

"What do you mean, you don't have a hat?"

"I don't have a hat and I don't think I can come."

"Well, what happened to your hats?"

"They're all old and I can't travel without a hat. I'm sorry."

"Can I get you a hat?"

"I guess I can try to see if there is something still open."

"I'll call you back."

My first response was to call my mother to make sure that these claims were legitimate. I couldn't imagine that my father would decide at the last minute not to come because he did not have a hat. As I thought about it, though, the symbolism was quite apparent, particularly for black men. I do remember seeing my grandfather, my father, and other black men wearing hats at all formal ceremonies. During that time, whether they were going to a wedding, funeral, or some other significant event, a hat was always worn. This experience was somewhat new to me, since I had never worn a hat to a formal event. In fact, my interest in hats was quite the opposite. When I wore a hat it was always for a political reason. The hats I wore at the time were beanie caps, skull caps, or some other kind that black men wore that had different symbolism. It was the kind of hat worn by the Black Panther Party or Student Non-Violent Coordinating Committee or similar events. However, the distinction in why we wore them did not dawn on me until I realized how serious he was about not coming.

With the help of my mother, I called a local department store, convinced them to agree to let me use my credit card long-distance, and allow my father to come down to the store to purchase a hat. He went down, bought a hat that was charged to me, and then told me that he would be coming.

My father arrived in Washington, participated in the ceremony, and had a great time. He was able to meet all of my colleagues, observe Justice Thurgood Marshall in the Supreme Court, and talk to his brother about forty years of experiences that they had not been able to share personally. It was also a wonderful occasion for me. I became closer to my father and was able to understand, to a greater extent, some of his reluctance to come forward in life. While sharing stories of growing up with his brother in Birmingham, they were much more candid when they spoke together about the discrimination of the many years of Jim Crow. For the first time I began to fully understand my father's decisions not to come to my high school, college, and law school graduations. He was a black man with a great deal of pride, with very little formal education, who would be in circumstances that, while he would celebrate my success, others would question his. How would he answer the question "What do you do?" How would he respond when someone said, "How do you explain your son's success?" I believe that the pressure was unbearable, and in some sense explains his reluctance to play such a public role.

The circumstance is also full of ironies. I was proud to have had such a successful high school, college, and law school career and wanted to share that with those who made it possible. While my mother readily accepted the invitation to attend these events and expected to be there, my father never had.

As a result of his visit to Washington in 1983, we became stronger. While we were still father and son, I also
think we developed a much more intimate friendship.
That was also witnessed by the fact that my father expressed great love for my children and wife, and got
along well with my family.

Shortly after the graduation ceremony, I had a conversation with my father about the days when we used to
watch baseball games. And he again expressed how
much he enjoyed the California teams, particularly the
San Francisco Giants. I knew that he had an interest in
the Giants because when I played little league baseball,
even though he was not living with us, he would wake
us up on those mornings we caught the team bus to go
to San Francisco to watch the games. The buses would
leave from Merced at seven, and our father would call us
at five. He would pick us up and take us to meet the other
little league team members, and watch us head off to San
Francisco. When we returned, he was there to make sure
that we got home. He would also quiz us about the details of the game, to see if we had watched it closely. He
would have watched on television or listened on the radio, and would know whether or not we had really paid
attention.

As we talked later in life about those games, my father
revealed to me, for the first time, that he had never been
to Candlestick Park himself. I was startled to hear this. I
asked him if he would be interested in going, and he
indicated that he would. Several months after my father's
visit to Washington, I took him and my family and a niece
and nephew to a Giants game. As is normally the case, I
tried to get seats high in the grandstand so that we could

see the entire field. I noticed how reluctant my father was, then in his seventies, to sit in that section and his increasing discomfort. I asked him whether he was enjoying the game. He indicated that he was, but he had a fear of heights. I had never been aware of this, and immediately switched our seats down to a lower section of the stadium. We enjoyed watching the game, and he certainly enjoyed spending the time with his grandchildren.

After that game I continued to talk with my father on a regular basis about a host of issues. He seemed much more engaging, and the relationship grew stronger.

Less than year later, I received a call from my mother early one morning. The coincidence is that it was on March 17, 1994, St. Patrick's Day. She told me that my father had gone to the hospital on an emergency basis the night before, and had a heart attack. He had not suffered much and died quite quickly. It was shocking and painful to hear. What was most amazing is that it came at the point when my father and I were just beginning to develop a special relationship.

As I prepared for his funeral in Merced, California, I was reminded of all the warm moments we'd had in the last year of his life, and also the ironic contradiction of events many years before. I began to understand much more about him, and felt cheated that he was no longer with us. It renewed my sense of what it means to appreciate the importance of parents, and make sure that they know that you love them when they are here rather than after they are gone. Kevin Costner had to build a baseball field to have his heroes come to Iowa. I simply had to buy a hat to have mine come to me.

Thaddeus Goodavage

Are You My Father?

Thaddeus Goodavage is a pseudonym for a freelance writer.

"Fathering" has saved my life. Twice. The first time it was by getting a father, and the second time it was by becoming a father. For at both points in my life, fathering—that need and potential in my soul to father and be fathered, had to be nurtured and made real. Initially, I desperately needed a father-caretaker, and later I was so paralyzed with feelings of such a deep loneliness and worthlessness that I was unable to understand why I was a valuable person and why I should try to remain alive. Having kids is just one attempt at solidity during this type of moment. My children—all three of my young sons—affirmed and continue to affirm two fundamental yet competing and sometimes contradictory impulses: my lifelong desire to be parented properly and my need to know another person with whom I have a genetic link.

I was an adopted child. Twice. My first parents (who liberated me from state care when I was seven months old), died tragically a year later. My second parents (who liberated me from state care for the second time when I was two years old) remain my loving, sacrificing, beautiful black parents. Their caretaking, though rich with practical support and ripe with an incredible caring love, did not leave space for sensitivity to the specific needs of an adopted child. I marched through life with them with just one discussion of the reality of our relationship: at seven years old a friend with whom I happened to be playing some funny hair-combing game, asked me, in the presence of my mother, why I did not look like or have hair like either of my parents. My mother, interrupting, suggested that I looked a whole lot like my father (which was somewhat true). After my friend's departure, she immediately pulled me into her room and told me that I was adopted and that I should never let anyone else know this fact because it would cause "embarrassment" to our family. Thus began my history of harboring the secret of my beginnings, my family, and myself.

My history and its hidden secrets, however, are merely a minor part of a very old narrative of concealment. Many veils separate struggling subjects from their fundamental selves. My best friend and love of my life has convinced me recently to begin to discover why I am who I am, to confront the secrets I have been complicit in keeping. I have always known I should have been doing this kind of work—and I have done some of it, but I have always been afraid to do it in certain areas. I was not sure that I could manage my secrets. Yet with patterns of pain so clear to me, a history so crowded with brokenness, and a perspicacious partner, I realized I must confront the reality of myself. None of us should dwell in secrets.

I have always felt incredibly alone. This feeling has much to do with who I am as a father, a friend, a person, a lover, and a son. My need to face and conquer this loneliness—and the feelings of meaninglessness from which it naturally derives—takes me on this journey of discovery. I grab my partner's hand and begin (this work is too hard to do alone, so bring a friend—a good, committed friend—along). I lift the veil to find and save myself, my sons, and Love.

This is by no means an argument to support the Enlightenment mythology that "knowledge is king" or that "the Truth"—a so-called "bringing everything to light"—is the only way. It is merely an attempt, and probably a flawed one, at improving myself and hopefully the quality of the lives of a few others.

One component of getting under the veil, one way of exploring my own incompleteness, means understanding how I was fathered. Looking at my dad's story before our initial encounter, however, requires developing new sensibilities. My father has told me little of his past. This proud man somehow made the choice to spare me the trauma of having to negotiate the pain that his stories would possibly engender. Yet to find myself through him, I need to be able to understand him as a man—his issues, his circumstances, his insights—in short, I need to know him. Then I have to become sensitive to his experience as a father—the father of an adopted child.

Fathering an adopted child is an underinvestigated phenomenon with its own specific set of built-in complications, issues, and joys. The traditional ritual and approach to fathering a biological son is, in some ways, a grand stroke of the ego, for it allows an older male to bond—at least physically—with what he both used to be and what he possibly could become. Many African-American fathers of sons use the fathering process as a terrain upon which to equip and train young warriors to deal with the harrowing and horrifying aspects of white supremacy. In effect, much of this training is a reaction to the life of the father; his experience in the world dictates how he orients his son in it. This is, naturally, what parenting is about. Yet this premise normally requires three assumptions that, if not considered thoroughly, can make the parent-child experience an incredibly problematic one. These assumptions are: (1) the parent's own childhood, and his or her recollection of it, are sufficient basis from which to parent twenty odd years later (e.g., children who occupy an elevated class status based on their parents' sacrifices have a quite different context for growing up than their parents—how does one parent with this in mind?); (2) there is a similar personality style, intellectual style, and conception of the world between parent and child (sometimes a child's personality is egregiously incompatible with a parental style, and in this scenario, it becomes difficult for parents to impart a certain kind of knowledge); (3) the child has exonerated the parental perspective as normative (which requires various other previous subconscious acceptances from child to parent—a certain kind of awe, respect, trust, and uncritical acceptance).

My dad's commitment to my developing autonomy and independence was strong. Yet both of us found out later that the normal assumptions he was operating on (which I described above) were not compatible with who I was. Maybe his parenting style would have worked if I was genetically his. That way I might have been predisposed to the predilections that make him successful as a parent. Maybe if we had shared heredity, I would have a personality more like his so that I could have dealt more easily with how and who he was. Yet we went on, struggling to be parent and child without directly grappling with these issues. I went on feeling alone.

Dad would help forge my sense of survival in the world by various tests and games at home, by suggesting I join Boy Scouts, and by one of his favorite wintertime "army-like" survival games. For this "game" he would drive me blindfolded to an open field, lead me out of the car, guide me to the middle of the field, and leave me there to fend for myself. I would have to find my way home on my own (negotiating animals, streams, brush, and various other natural forces). Later, Dad would convince me that he had never left me, and that I was always in his sight as I cried and wandered around searching for my way home, some warmth, and sometimes food. But I never felt his presence; I always felt incredibly alone. He was very good at hiding. Or I was bad at seeing him nearby.

Fathering a biological son provides a certain space to celebrate maleness intergenerationally and genetically. In the elite context of biological father-son relationships, maleness—that sacrosanct quality grounded on falsely constructed notions of power—moves along uncriticized, as a father essentially remakes himself in another who closely resembles him.

Adoption means that this resemblance is not present. This father, no matter how hard he tries, is confronted with the "other" as son. A certain kind of distance is, then, a built-in component of adoption. This distance becomes a site of anxiety, and the father, who only wanted to uncritically pass on his manhood to someone like himself, finds himself facing a young male he does not know. Adoptive Father looks desperately for himself in his son, and he cannot find himself. Adoptee son looks desperately for himself in his father, to no avail. Both, probably, are tremendously lonely.

My dad was a boxer, a weight lifter, and an all-around tough guy during his youth. I was a skinny, sissy-like kid (which he constantly reminded me of), afraid of every insect, animal, and person I encountered. After he concluded that I was lagging way behind in my physical development, he decided to help the developmental process along. He sentenced me to twenty-five push-ups a night. Every day at ten o'clock I had to go into the living room, where he would be alone watching television, lie at the feet of his Laz-y Boy chair, and do the push-ups while he watched for form and counted. I never could do more than four. He would yell and moan about how weak I was and how I wasn't improving until, after wobbly completing number five (I always cheated and used my knees on this one) he would send me directly to bed and make me turn the lights out. My constant feelings of being deeply alone heightened, I would get under my covers and read with a flashlight. Then I would turn my transistor radio on softly and place it under my pillow. I would click the light off, and the music would carry me to sleep. Sometimes I wish I still had that radio.

Adoption demands a profound reconstruction of the notions of father, son, parent, and family. This different type of psychic orientation to fatherhood is, it seems to me, of some import, and, sadly, no one talks about this. Families affected by adoption have gone through (even before the adoption occurs), critically or subconsciously, the process of turning the traditional notions of family upside down. They have developed a way of gaining a new self-understanding in relation to these terms, of re-defining these traditional notions, and creating a structure based on their newly arrived-at understanding of what constitutes a family. It is important to recognize this deeply radical shift in consciousness that my parents, par-ticularly my father (for the purposes of this essay), had to contend with, for this helps me to lift the veils.

What really happens psychically to individuals in a culture that has very fixed and unchanging notions of family, parenthood, etc., when they realize they cannot/ do not fit into these traditional conceptions? How does one build a family when he begins from a different start-ing point than most other families? How do black people, already viewed as not fully human in our culture, live with this fact and still work to construct a family, partic-ularly when that family is one with adopted children? How does a black woman, whose body and skin are de-spised and devalued in our society, come to terms with the fact that she cannot do the one thing that all women are supposed to do, which is to produce offspring? How is her womanhood affected by this, and if she decides to construct a family with adopted children, how are these issues going to manifest in her mothering? How does a black man, already disaffirmed and demasculated by the wider society, affirm his own manhood when he cannot create, produce, or sustain anything, even children? What kind of father will he be? How will his legacy as a father affect a twice-abandoned, twice-chosen child? Why have I always felt so alone? These are just a few of the ques-tions with which I grapple.

Some of these issues and their ramifications are clearer to me now because I am older and because I know what having biological children, sons, has meant for me. I feel sorry for my parents who could not—and I feel guilty for being a daily reminder to them *that* they could not—have biological children. The anxieties, fears, paranoias, strengths, and insights that have resulted from my early trauma I think I can contend with. Yet when I think of my mom and dad, I wonder how they deal with these cruel, hard facts that none of us has ever talked about. They have never tried to lift the veil. I can only surmise that their own deep self-sacrifices have reaped only partial benefits in their soul. Yet I must appreciate their sacrifices and try to imagine how important the fact that fathering an adopted son is less a stroke of the ego than an exercise in commitment and sacrifice. I deeply appreciate these sacrifices, and given my own history around these issues, I marvel at my dad's constitution around them.

My father and mother, hardworking providers that they were, never verbally articulated that they loved me; they expected that their sacrifices would say it for them (in many ways, they did). For Depression-era Negroes who had undergone the migration northward, the movement to integration, and so many watershed historical moments regarding race, gender, economy, and technology that it is mind-boggling, this type of emotional calm and understatement is understandable, maybe even typical behavior. In addition, given each of my parents' family histories and issues and the fact that I was adopted, maybe this is quite acceptable behavior. But I still wonder, when I say "I love you" to my children and my partner (not their mother) every day (and quietly wait for them to repeat it to me), what would have been different in my life, if anything, had I gotten the opportunity to hear my parents tell me they loved me with some regularity during my childhood and adolescent years? Would I have felt so profoundly alone if they had verbally and physically articulated an unconditional love more clearly? Or was I already destined to feel alone based on being adopted, my emotional makeup, etc.? I wish I knew.

When I lift the veil of my family life I am faced with the fundamental question: Why do I feel so lonely? Which, phrased in a more useful way, would read: *am I loved, am I worthy of love, and will I be left alone in the world without love?* These are the questions with which I struggle most and which my existence seeks desperately to reconcile.

All of us are looking for love. Whether or not we are able to participate in a family where unconditional love is at the foundation of our experience is of significance, we find ourselves adjusting to this foundational experience during our entire lives. Growing up, I never knew how alone I was because I only knew being alone. My soul longed for attention, acceptance, and affirmation, and I engaged in the full spectrum of behavior to get this attention and affirmation. As an infant I remember crying a lot, never letting my "mother" out of my sight, not being able to sleep, trying to please my parents as much as possible (typical behavior of an adopted child). As I grew older, my quest for acceptance and affirmation made me try to be perfect; I figured, "If I listen, I will make everyone happy and everyone will love me." I did excellently in school, I obeyed my parents. I was still, in spite of much public attention and high community regard, very lonely.

Of course, no one is perfect no matter how hard they try to be, and after a while my attempts to please my parents in order to receive their affirmation began to fail. I could not be all that they seemed to want or need. My dad wanted me to be physically stronger and more of a tough guy, and he came to resent my affinity for white people, classical music, and books. His own experience and "success" in the world (he went from the underclass to the lower middle-class—the only one of five children in an alcoholic and extremely light-skinned Negro family to do so) and his desire to protect me so that I could "succeed" informed him in ways that forced him to undermine my interests. In his mind, he was trying his best to look out for his son. I was quite confused because I knew him to be (and still do) the man of the most dignity and integrity I have ever known. His commitment to staying true to his beliefs, to not compromising in the face of personal gain, to representing himself in a clean, well-groomed manner, to maintaining a connection to troubled children and the less fortunate, is profound and significant. He is the most deeply dutiful man I know, but he would never take me to, or attend, any of my rehearsals or concerts. He would not help or support me doing my homework, and he would oftentimes not even speak to my white friends. I found refuge from my isolation in music and books. I was, in the eyes of the general public, a wonderfully successful and talented kid. No one could see my torment.

In hindsight, I realize that I could have maneuvered differently in the face of his issues. As a youngster, however, I did not know better, so instead of loving him hard in spite of his issues, digging in my heels, and fighting him, I displaced him. My sense of already being alone, and fears and feelings of not being adequately loved informed me in ways that made me pull out of the relationship—my dad no longer existed in my psychic world. This displacement of him drove him to deeper anger because it meant that I refused to respect his position as provider. For me, this was easy because we really had nothing in common anyway, except for the same roof: our bodies were quite different, our sensibilities were greatly different, and our interests and intellects seemed to have no common reference point. I was still deeply lonely; my move away from him did not change that.

I moved on. I found other male role models and venerated them with a vengeance, ones who (unlike my dad) respected my mind (my teachers), appreciated my love of music and poetry (my conductors and tutors) and who seemed to feel impressed by my talents and potentials as an individual. My father, it seemed, began to despise me. And, worse than that, I still felt a deep internal loneliness.

But this is not just another narrative about an old black man who could not love his son. The way my father understood his role as father and the way he was able (or unable) to love me is the point here. There is much to be said about the way he understands responsibility, commitment, and stability. I cannot criticize him for the man that he is. I can only hope to understand myself better by acknowledging his impact on me. Yet I realize that I long for a closeness with him that I never had at the same time that I recognize that why I feel like I want to be close to him may not have anything to do with him.

I long to be fathered, by anybody. So I have found

numerous other father figures to mentor and "raise" me. Strong, black, thoughtful, soulful, disciplined, sophisticated brothers who could both relate to who and where I was. I have, and had always had, a "successful" existence. Yet I always feel so scared and alone. I long to be loved. Most important, *I long for the type of unconditional love that I seem to have never been able to explicitly find.* I long to not be lonely and alone.

This longing leads me to be incredibly sensitive, giving, kind, comforting, warm, and gentle. In intimate relations I create an atmosphere of safety and caring that is quite attractive to most women. This, in addition to my public presentation, commitment to elegance, and thoughtfulness, lead me, in some estimations, to be considered attractive. In fact, my loneliness and neediness was so profound and, concomitantly, my giving so enormous, that I got married quite young. When I immediately felt abandoned in the marriage and all alone once again (she didn't want me when she refused to allow me to continue to entirely consume her thoughts, actions, and desires) I became quite depressed. My hopes of having a partner to fulfill me now gone, I did not know where to turn. Then it became clear: I realized that the only way for me to get the kind of unconditional love I needed to stay alive would be to get it from fathering a child. We had a son, and I got all of the unconditional love possible. Also, and just as important, my son provided me with a chance to safely give all the unconditional love that I had to give, plus more. I was fulfilled.

Having a child conquered my sense of being entirely alone in the world. Here was someone who was entirely dependent on me, who I had unlimited access to, who could not leave me. My life had been saved. Finally, I had established a link, a bond, an unbreakable connection, with someone else in the world. This worked incredibly well for a while, then three things happened. The first had to do with my father. Having a family, in some ways, made me feel more like him than I had ever imagined I would. Certainly, I had my own parenting style, but when I felt like I began to act like him, I became afraid that I would become him and I needed to change direction quickly. Second, I began to lift the very delicately laid veil around my biological parents and found out about my biological father. And third, because of the first two reasons, a new baby (and another on the way), and my wife's own history and issues, my home life became deeply disharmonious. I moved out—just far enough to escape the craziness, but not too far to be without my sons—up to this point the only source of genetic perpetuity and unconditional love that I had ever known. Let me return, however, to the second most impactful occurrence I mentioned above.

Part of the secret around being adopted I had actually never resisted. Until the time I was twenty-five I had told only three people about my status in the world. Ever. When my well-intended wife suggested I find my biological parents for medical reasons having to do with our child, it all came back in a rush. What I had been doing with my new baby son had not been done with, or for, me. I decided to find my biological parents. During adolescence I would frequently dream about a rich, glamorous biological heritage. I would imagine somehow bumping into people on the street who looked so much like me that I would immediately recognize them to be my real family. They would also recognize me and take me home with them to some amazing castle-like home and be the family I always imagined. Needless to say, this never happened.

Uncovering my biological roots was much easier and more difficult than I expected—it was a process that took many years. After numerous phone calls, letters, and discussions with family welfare workers to private investigators, I received a telephone call one day from someone claiming to be my biological brother. He was the second of six children to be born from the woman who had also borne me. His voice sounded a little bit like mine.

I talked to him for an hour. He knew about me. His mother had told him and all of his brothers and sisters that she had had me and had given me away and that I was, she hoped, safely placed somewhere in the universe. She told them how hard it was to have a child and not know him. Every year she and her children would celebrate my birthday. She told them that my father (they all had different fathers) was a kind man who had died some time ago.

I told him to tell his mother that I was not angry with her (the fear she had articulated to him as the reason she had not called me) and that I would love to speak to her. But I was torn. Here I was betraying the sacred bond that my parents had worked so incredibly hard to establish with me. I did not want to betray this bond, yet I was intrinsically unhappy with my relationship with my parents, I was curious about my biological inheritance, and I was excited about the possibilities of meeting the source of my genetic makeup. She called the next day.

Separated by histories, too many issues, twenty-seven

years, hundreds of thoughts, thousands of miles, and millions of tears between us, we came together. When I first heard her voice on the phone, I was incredibly excited, scared, and moved. It was one of the most profound sounds that I have *ever* experienced. I talked with her. I flirted with her. I charmed her. Most of all, I tried to win her over. In retrospect, I guess I wanted her to *want* to be my mother. I wanted her to hold me and treat me with the tenderness she was supposed to provide for me at birth. The next day I flew to see her.

Trains, planes, and a rental car finally brought me face to face with the woman whom I had grown inside of. When I saw her nose, her hair, her chin, her ears, her face, her shape, her walk, her laugh, I felt a different kind of link to the earth. I felt a different kind of link to myself. We communicated with the movements and gestures and feelings and hopes and sadnesses that only we knew. She knew me. This was quite a significant experience for me, and I felt as if my loneliness was fading. For a moment.

My biological father, I found out after this long journey to find my mother, was said not to be alive anymore. Yet in his day he'd had a reputation as being one of the most renowned small-time pimps, hustlers, and charmers in his community. My genetic roots are as follows: repeated sexual abuse by her parents motivated my biological mother to run away at the age of fourteen. Survival on the streets meant that she became a prostitute, a drug addict, and an alcoholic. My biological father was her thirty-three-year-old, thrice-married pimp who, according to her, also fell in love with her. She got pregnant with his child.

They tried to abort me. Twice. They agreed that she was too young to be a mother and that the circumstances would make it impossible for me to grow up healthy. The first time she took pills. Two weeks later, she tried a coat hanger. With nowhere to go, after her man went back to his wife, this fourteen-year-old girl and chaotic home of mine, dragged herself back to her parents. These cruel, sexually abusive parents of hers, who had driven all of their children to depression (my biological mother's brother killed himself at eighteen), refused to let her in. All alone, she went to her church. Those good Catholics helped her deliver me and immediately handed me over to the state during the first ten seconds of life. We both cried.

Racism has affected me more deeply than most. Twice. The first time (which I realized only much later) was when my biological mother's parents would not let her back in their house when she was pregnant. My biological mother is white. My biological father is black. The second time was when I found this out.

Much like the children's story in which the baby bird falls out of its nest, begins a frantic search for his mother, and is finally saved by her (and fed by her) after confronting various other entities to ask them if they were his mother, I felt like I was rescued. I had found her. She was like me. But she was white. When I saw her skin, her hair, her lips, her nose—I studied them. I looked at her so closely, as if I had a microscope, and I saw her whiteness in a way that I had never seen whiteness before. I saw it in relation to me.

I had never imagined that I was not a black person. That is to say, I never thought that I might have a white biological parent. For some strange reason, it actually never crossed my mind. Now I had to confront the fact that I was biracial, that I did not comfortably and easily fit into any race category, and that I had been living a lie. Or had I? What constitutes one's racial identity? Was I really black or not, and how did it matter? I was still lonely. The truths I had been taught were now crumbling at my feet. Veils were being lifted. I was not feeling safe.

Moreover, the stories my biological mother fed me were much more impactful than I thought, especially when she told me about my father. She told me how he talked, how he walked, what he thought about, how he engaged the world. I didn't tell her then, but much of what she said he said, I had said before. Much of what she said he thought, I had thought before. Much of what she said he did, I had done before. I found myself in my biological father—pimp, hustler, charmer, social activist, sensitive thinker, sometimes poet, incredible dresser, musician, neighborhood conversationalist, all around cool brother. My God. Who was I? How could I reconcile him with me? The recognition that one's genes are descended from a criminal father (and "crazy" mother—who was, and for a long while had been, a hooker), especially a father who you existentially resemble, is enough to confuse you about yourself.

I had nowhere to turn but inward. My two fathers pulled at my soul. Responsibility and commitment tugged me in one direction, and the smooth-operator mentality pulled me into the other. I got a divorce.

My past feelings of being alone, of being homeless, and of being abandoned were now at an all-time high. I felt that I had nowhere to turn and felt that nobody really loved me. Except for my children. I had so much to give them, I wanted to have them around me all of the time. Yet their mother would not allow that. The only link to the type of unconditional love I cherished was now being taken from me. I tried to get joint custody of my children. I lost.

Could I ever find and sustain the type of love that I felt I needed? I hoped so, but I decided to stop looking for it.

Love found me in the form of a realization. That realization was that I needed help. I needed to lift the veils to find the truth, to be open about myself, to grapple with the truth, use it as best as I could to improve myself, to ultimately be happy with the person that I am. Love was to start the process of self-discovery that I am now beginning. Asking myself about my family life, asking myself about how I was fathered, forcing myself to remember my pain is about my beginning to heal. I figured out some things alone, and healing has started, yet my deepest issues—those of intimacy—could be touched only with the help of an incredibly talented partner who could both love me for who I am, yet gently prod me into confronting the painful secrets of my past and, at the same time, convince me that I was safe with her. I found the self I had tried to run away from only with her love and support.

She claims to have willed me to her. I searched for her for practically a year. Some force greater than ourselves brought us together. Our link has been transformative and powerful.

As veils have been lifted, discoveries have been made. Underneath the veils I began to see how my history limits me from reaching my potential in the world, particularly as an intimate partner (because the most intimate historical space for me—my relationship with my mother and father—was so unusual). In some parts of intimacy, I am amazing—my deep sensitivities are incredibly useful. In other parts of intimacy, these same sensitivities and fears of being alone are paralyzing for both me and my partner. When she leaves to go to work, something I know she has to and loves to do, I feel deeply alone on the inside —like I am not being chosen. When she says something, anything, my mind constantly peruses her claim, looking for ways in which she is saying she might want to leave me. I am so afraid.

My partner has been patiently helping me see how my fears limit me and us and how they are linked, somehow, to my past. I continue to work on changing my issues from various vantage points—reading, writing, counseling, thinking, etc., yet I realize that I am, fundamentally, who I am—and that I cannot change that.

Every day I try to get under another veil, to get back to a truth, no matter how painful, and grapple with the me that I am. Doing this has shown me that both of my "fathers" have affected me in profoundly different ways. I blame neither of these noble men totally for my issues —circumstance has created me. Like everyone else, I have some wonderful qualities and some problems. I try to work on my problems so that I can be more loving, happier, and more able to give and provide for others.

Allowing myself to think openly and critically about my fathers brings me back to me. From this place I can do the liberating work of lifting the veils and uncovering the secrets that have caused me, and others, problems and pain. From this place I can discover myself in all of my richness—the good and the bad. From the truths of my fathers—and how I was fathered—I can understand myself better as father and convert my issues into assets to help me to be successful in my intimate life, my parental life, my life as a son, a friend, a writer—everywhere. Here I stand at the beginning of that process.

All parenting requires a certain degree of heroism. I struggle, and ask you to struggle, to be the superheroes we need to be.

· A NOTE ON THE TYPE ·

The typeface used in this book is a version of Palatino, originally designed in 1950 by Hermann Zapf (b. 1918), one of the most prolific contemporary type designers, who has also created Melior and Optima. Palatino was first used to set the introduction of a book of Zapf's hand lettering, in an edition of eighty copies on Japan paper handbound by his wife, Gudrun von Hesse; the book sold out quickly and Zapf's name was made. (Remarkably, the lettering had actually been done when the self-taught calligrapher was only twenty-one.) Intended mainly for "display" (title pages, headings), Palatino owes its appearance both to calligraphy and the requirements of the cheap German paper at the time—perhaps why it is also one of the best-looking fonts on low-end computer printers. It was soon used to set text, however, causing Zapf to redraw its more elaborate letters.